Joni Seager, Professor and Chair of Global Studies at Bentley University in Boston, is a geographer and global policy expert. She has achieved international acclaim for her work in feminist environmental policy analysis, the international status of women, and global political economy. She is the author of many books, including four editions of the award-winning *Atlas of Women in the World,* two editions of *The State of the Environment Atlas*, and *Earth Follies: Coming to Feminist Terms With the Global Environmental Crisis.* She is co-author, with Cynthia Enloe, of *The Real State of America Atlas.* Joni has been an active consultant with the United Nations on several gender and environmental policy projects, including consulting with the United Nations Environmental Programme on integrating gender perspectives into their work on disasters and early warning systems, and with UNESCO on gender in water policy.

Praise for previous editions:

"Here is the innovative atlas no thoughtful person, male or female, should be without. The aim is facts, not a manifesto. A wealth of fascinating information."
The Washington Post

"A fascinating atlas: A compilation of facts about women's status, work, health, education, and personal freedom across the globe, it is not only an invaluable reference book, but also throws up questions about why a woman's lot is not as good as a man's."
The Independent

"Much of the plethora of information contained within the pages is shocking. A fascinating document, and an extremely valuable one."
Independent Magazine

"An appealing idea, imaginatively executed."
Times Higher Education Supplement

"A major reference tool. The atlas format and highly original colorful statistical illustrations make this a book as enjoyable as it is important."
Library Journal

"No-one wishing to keep a grip on the reality of the world should be without these books." *International Herald Tribune*

Available now:

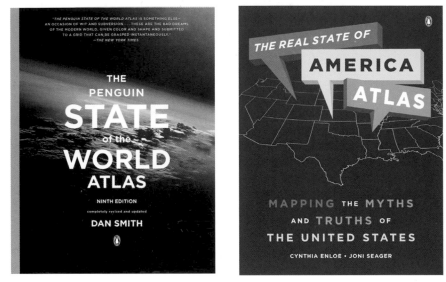

Available 2015:

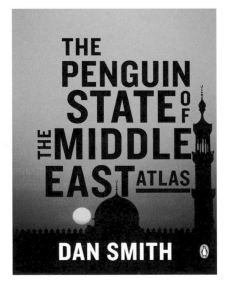

"Invaluable…I would not be without the complete set on my own shelves."
Times Educational Supplement

"Fascinating and invaluable." *The Independent*

"A new kind of visual journalism." *New Scientist*

The Penguin Atlas of
WOMEN
IN THE WORLD

Completely Revised and Updated
Fourth Edition

Joni Seager

PENGUIN BOOKS

PENGUIN BOOKS

Published by the Penguin Group
Penguin Group (USA) LLC
375 Hudson Street
New York, New York 10014

USA | Canada | UK | Ireland | Australia | New Zealand | India | South Africa | China
penguin.com
A Penguin Random House Company

This fourth edition first published in Penguin Books 2009

Penguin paperback ISBN 978-0-14-311451-2

Edited and coordinated by Elizabeth Wyse and Candida Lacey
with Jannet King and Martine McDonagh
Designed by Isabelle Lewis and Corinne Pearlman
Maps and graphics by Isabelle Lewis

Printed on paper produced from sustainable sources.
Printed and bound in Hong Kong through Lion Production
Under the supervision of Bob Cassels, The Hanway Press, London.

5 7 9 10 8 6

Contents

Part Four: Body Politics   44

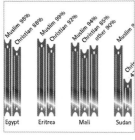

Part Five: Work   60

Part Six: To Have and To Have Not

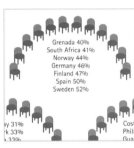

Introduction

There have been some remarkable improvements in the state of women since the first edition of this atlas was published in 1986. Improvements in women and girls' literacy and education top the list of global success stories; women have won voting rights and the right to hold public office in all but a small handful of countries; most of the world's governments have signed international treaties committed to women's rights. The importance of such gains should not be underestimated.

But, overall, the "success story" list is depressingly short. Many women around the world have experienced an absolute decline in the quality of their life over the past decade. Improvements in one place are not necessarily transferable to other places: we remain a world divided. The globalizing new world economy is based largely on exploiting "flexible" markets of underpaid workers; women's participation in this new world economy is not an unalloyed sign of progress. The global gap between rich and poor has widened, and there are now more women and men living in dire poverty than a decade ago; women remain the poorest of the poor, everywhere. Around the world, "structural adjustment" policies coordinated and imposed by rich-world governments have plunged country after country into social and economic crisis; it is women who have borne the cost of managing the economic fallout. Wars have wracked several countries; in Afghanistan, Iraq, the Congo, Sudan, and Chechnya (among many others), millions of people are living under regimes of armed terror in wrenching conditions. Women bear a special burden of these wars, including horrific mass rapes, erosion of their rights, and the unrelenting demands of sustaining families and households in the midst of chaos. In former socialist countries, women are paying an especially high price for the transition to a free-market economy and society: everywhere this transition brings with it skyrocketing rates of violence and sexual exploitation, sharp increases in women's unemployment, an abrupt end to government support for healthcare, childcare, and housing, and even less representation for women in the emerging economic and political elites than they had in the old regimes. Religious fundamentalism and a resurgent conservative intolerance threaten women's rights in a wide range of states – and in a wide range of ways – across the globe. Millions of women around the world live their daily lives as little more than chattels. Large-scale systems of enslavement and oppression of women, including, prominently, sex trafficking, are flourishing.

Where is the outrage? Women do not automatically share in broad social advances: a rising tide does not necessarily raise all boats unless there is a commitment to do so. Feminists have often warned that gains in women's empowerment should not be taken for granted: they are fragile and reversible and always under pressure. This warning has never been more pertinent. At best we can say that from Pakistan to the USA, from Russia to Sierra Leone, the halls and hallmarks of power remain remarkably unperturbed by the oppression of women. At worst, evidence suggests that a remarkable number of governments in 2008 seem committed to turning back advances in women's autonomy.

Feminist organizing is stronger, more diverse, and more skilled than ever. International feminist networks have broken the isolation of women from one another; feminists everywhere are more informed about issues and perspectives from cultures and places outside their own immediate realm. Global feminist organizing is successfully redefining "human rights" to incorporate a broad agenda of "women's rights." Lesbian organizing has come out of the closet. As we enter the 21st century, we need public and civic leaders who will build on these feminist foundations to make unflinching real – not rhetorical – commitments to social justice for women.

As a feminist, I believe that social analysis and activism can be enriched by an international and broadly comparative perspective. However, working at a global scale also inevitably entails a degree of generalization that is troubling – and, indeed, that if left unexamined can undermine feminist analysis. The world of women is defined both by commonality and difference. Women everywhere share primary responsibility for having and rearing children, for forming and maintaining families, for contraception. They share too the lead in fighting for women's rights and other civil rights. Rich and poor, they also suffer rape, health traumas from illegal abortions, the degradation of pornography. Nonetheless, if we have learned anything from the feminist movement of the past three decades, it is that global generalizations must not be used to mask the very real differences that exist among women country by country, region by region. There are significant inequalities in wealth and in access to opportunities from place to place; these are then refracted and magnified by social signifiers such as race, ethnicity, age, or religious affiliation.

It is as a geographer that I have found a way to strike a balance between the demands of acknowledging both commonality and difference: at its best, mapping can simultaneously illuminate both. Mapping is a powerful tool; in showing not only what is happening but where, patterns are revealed on maps that would never be apparent in statistical tables or even in narratives. The similarities and differences, the continuities and contrasts among women around the world are perhaps best shown by mapping out – literally – their lives. It is my hope that this atlas raises as many questions as it provides answers.

There are many people without whom this atlas would not have been completed – or even started:

As always, I owe special thanks to my partner Cynthia Enloe, who never ceases to impress me with her analytical grasp, her intellectual generosity, her astonishing understanding of the state of women around the world, and her expansive sense of humor; without Cynthia's unflagging encouragement and support I would not be able to imagine doing this atlas.

I was supported in this edition by a team of skilled and dedicated students and colleagues who provided outstanding research assistance: many thanks to Sohaila Abdulali, Amy Freeman, Mabel Fu, Kristina Schmidt, and Michael Wilkerson. My thanks to Hunter College for providing research support funding and facilities.

Special thanks and credit go to Annie Olson, co-originator and co-author of the first edition.

The team at Myriad Editions, Candida Lacey, Isabelle Lewis, Corinne Pearlman and Elizabeth Wyse, once again performed astounding creative, editorial, and production feats to bring this project to fruition; they never fail to amaze me with their outstanding insight and generosity. Many thanks also to Jannet King and Martine McDonagh who put their shoulders to the wheel in the last stages to enable us to finish the atlas more or less on deadline! I miss the friendship and inspiration of Anne Benewick, the founder of Myriad; I wouldn't have arrived here at the fourth edition without her companionship on the journeys of earlier editions. As an independent small publisher, Myriad wedges open a space within which radical and creative ideas can flourish and we all benefit from their dedication and persistence. My special thanks to Myriad director, Bob Benewick, for his ongoing friendship and continuing dedication to the atlas series.

To my family, especially my mother Joan, my enduring thanks for their support, goodwill, and humour. To Gilda Bruckman and Judy Wachs, my extended family, I owe a great debt and thanks for the countless ways in which they enrich my life and expand my world. This atlas was further sustained by a wide network of friends, and I especially would like to thank: Julie Abraham, Alison Bernstein, Margaret Bluman, Mona Domosh, Madeline Drexler, Glen Elder, Tess Ewing, EJ Graff, Jane Knodell, Amy Lang, Wendy Luttrell, Louise Rice, Wendy Rosen, Robert Shreefter, Ellen Sippel, Laura Zimmerman. I am grateful for the inspiration and encouragement of my many friends and colleagues at the Center for New Words, the Geographic Perspectives on Women caucus, the University of Vermont, York University, Clark University, and Hunter College.

Many people provided assistance with specific maps or data, and I would like to particularly thank: Jenny Barrett; Lory Manning, Women's Research and Education Institute; Marilyn Dawson and Aparna Mehrotra at the United Nations; and Sophia Huyer, Women in Global Science and Technology.

Beyond these particular acknowledgements, I have never lost sight of the broader social and intellectual debt that I owe to the countless feminists – most unnamed and unrecognized – who, for years, and often at great personal cost, have been the only ones insisting that it is important to ask questions about where the women are. Without the collective support of women's movements around the globe, and the pathbreaking efforts of a persistent few, I would have neither the confidence nor the knowledge to undertake this atlas.

Joni Seager
Cambridge, Massachusetts

Part One

WOMEN IN THE WORLD

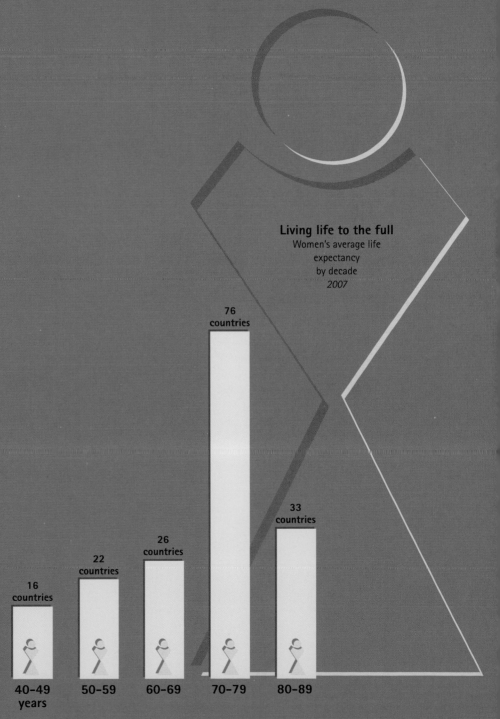

Living life to the full
Women's average life
expectancy
by decade
2007

76
countries

33
countries

26
countries

22
countries

16
countries

40–49
years

50–59

60–69

70–79

80–89

1 States Against Discrimination

Most of the world's governments are committed, on paper, to full equality for women. The Convention on the Elimination of All Forms of Discrimination Against Women (CEDAW), a UN treaty, was adopted in 1979 and came into force in 1981. It was the result of years of organizing by women, both within the United Nations and in dozens of countries around the world. The final impetus for drafting the treaty was the 1975 UN Women's Conference in Mexico.

CEDAW is not the first UN treaty concerning the status of women. Several earlier treaties on marriage rights, political rights, and trafficking set the stage for CEDAW, and remain important in their own right.

CEDAW establishes a universal set of standards and principles that are intended to serve as a template for shaping national policies towards the long-term goal of eliminating gender discrimination. Governments that ratify CEDAW are obliged to develop and implement policies and laws to eliminate discrimination against women within their country.

As with many international agreements, the practical effectiveness of CEDAW has been mixed. Many governments have ratified CEDAW without demonstrating much effort to comply with the treaty. Nonetheless, CEDAW establishes a platform of minimum expectations to which women's groups can – and do – hold governments accountable.

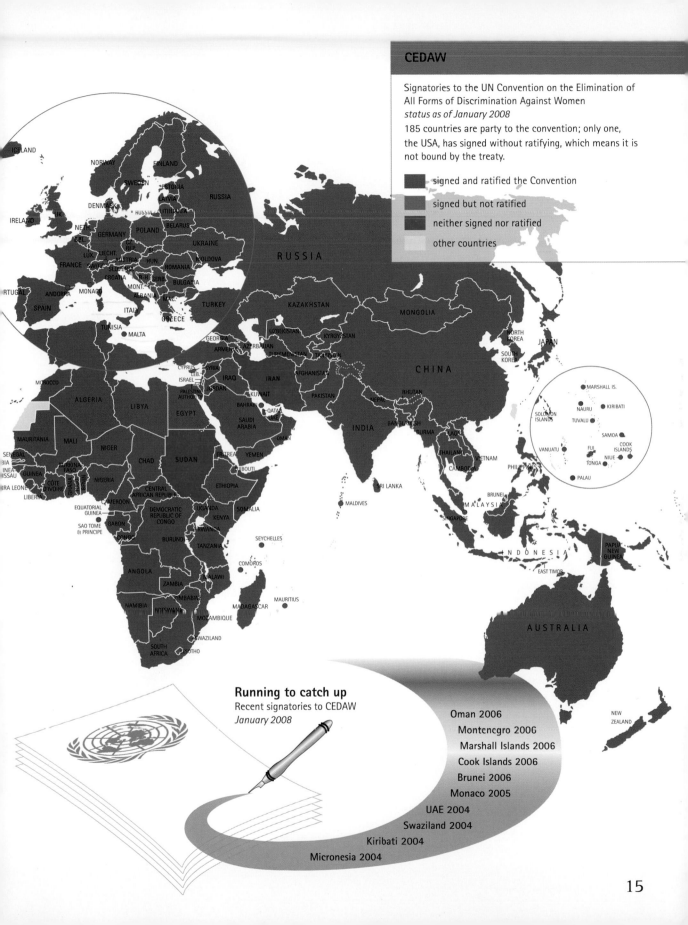

CEDAW

Signatories to the UN Convention on the Elimination of
All Forms of Discrimination Against Women
status as of January 2008
185 countries are party to the convention; only one,
the USA, has signed without ratifying, which means it is
not bound by the treaty.

- signed and ratified the Convention
- signed but not ratified
- neither signed nor ratified
- other countries

Running to catch up
Recent signatories to CEDAW
January 2008

Oman 2006
Montenegro 2006
Marshall Islands 2006
Cook Islands 2006
Brunei 2006
Monaco 2005
UAE 2004
Swaziland 2004
Kiribati 2004
Micronesia 2004

2 The State of Women

There is no easy way to compare the status of women around the world. Indeed, it is unwise to attempt to use any single lens through which to do so. Nonetheless, there are interesting ways to shed light on questions of overall status and general quality of life.

The Gender Development Index (GDI) offers one perspective. Developed by the United Nations Development Programme, the GDI assesses the extent to which countries have achieved success in three dimensions of human development: literacy, life expectancy, and income. These are then weighted according to gender disparities; the GDI thus ends up serving as a gender-sensitive measure of the state of a country's development.

Another lens through which to view the overall status of women is the Gender Gap Index (GGI), recently developed by the World Economic Forum. This index measures the relative equality between men and women in access to resources, regardless of the overall level of "development."

One of the points illustrated by both indices is that gender equality is, in part, a result of governmental commitments to equality principles and policies. For example, it is no coincidence that the Scandinavian countries rank very high in both indexes – these countries have adopted gender equality and women's empowerment as explicit national policies.

Life expectancy is an irreducible indicator of overall wellbeing. In most countries, women have an average life expectancy higher than their male counterparts, but for many of the world's women – and men – life is short and hard.

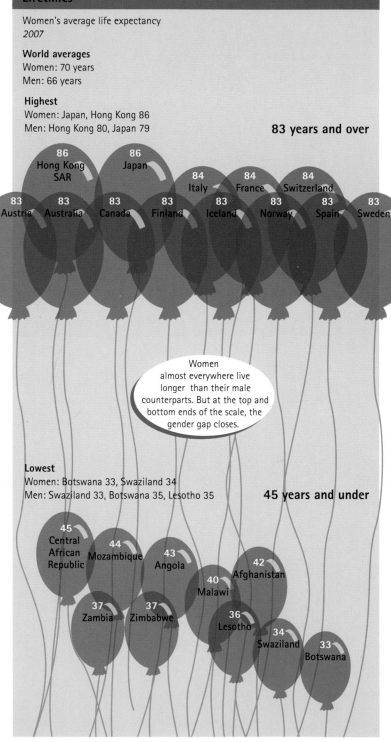

Lifetimes

Women's average life expectancy
2007

World averages
Women: 70 years
Men: 66 years

Highest
Women: Japan, Hong Kong 86
Men: Hong Kong 80, Japan 79

83 years and over

86 Hong Kong SAR
86 Japan
84 Italy
84 France
84 Switzerland
83 Austria
83 Australia
83 Canada
83 Finland
83 Iceland
83 Norway
83 Spain
83 Sweden

Women almost everywhere live longer than their male counterparts. But at the top and bottom ends of the scale, the gender gap closes.

Lowest
Women: Botswana 33, Swaziland 34
Men: Swaziland 33, Botswana 35, Lesotho 35

45 years and under

45 Central African Republic
44 Mozambique
43 Angola
42 Afghanistan
40 Malawi
37 Zambia
37 Zimbabwe
36 Lesotho
34 Swaziland
33 Botswana

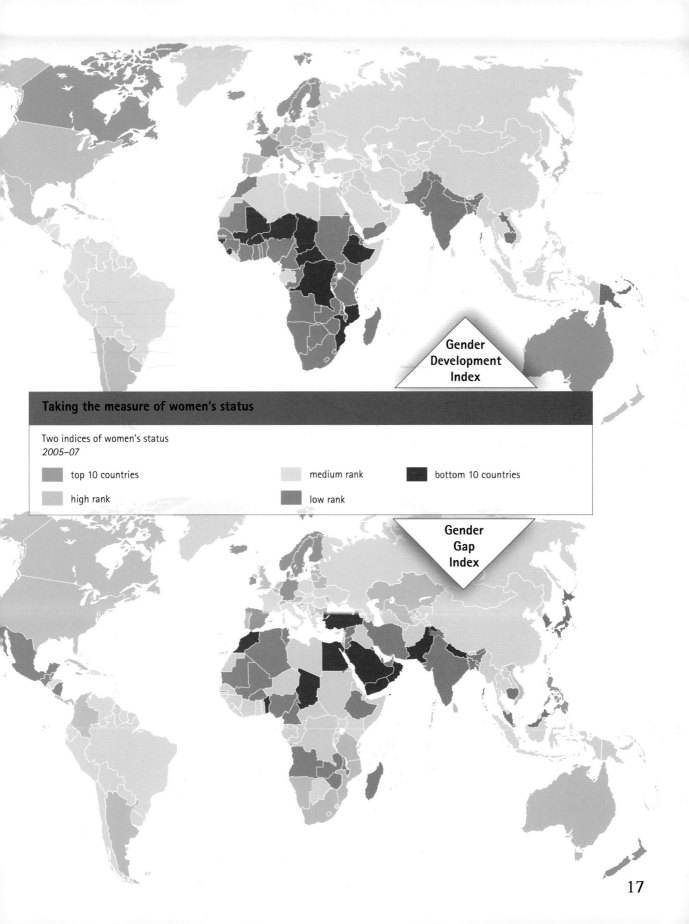

Gender
Development
Index

Taking the measure of women's status

Two indices of women's status
2005–07

top 10 countries

high rank

medium rank

low rank

bottom 10 countries

Gender
Gap
Index

3 In Their Place

As a broad political observation, we might say that women everywhere face *de facto* restrictions on their public presence, dress, and private and public behavior. But in many countries, "keeping women in their place" is a literal undertaking. Mobility and dress restrictions, enforced in a surprising number of countries, are rooted in standard patriarchal assumptions about men's right to control women, in potent combination with fundamentalist religious interpretations.

Women's rights are under increasing pressure from religious fundamentalism in many countries – Hindu fundamentalism in India, Christian fundamentalism in the USA, Roman Catholic in Croatia, Islamic in Algeria, are just some of the examples. The rising tide of fundamentalism is everywhere contested. Feminists have been especially active in challenging the legitimacy of fundamentalist proscriptions, and in offering alternative interpretations of religious texts.

Restrictions on women are in most cases symptomatic of wider human rights abuses and political repression. They are cultivated in a climate of widespread oppression that affects women and men in many ways.

CANADA

USA

USA: State legislatures enacted 301 anti-abortion measures between 1995 and 2001; 87% of all US counties are now not served by an abortion provider.

VENEZUELA

Venezuela: A provision in the penal code provides that an adult man guilty of raping an adult woman with whom he is acquainted can avoid punishment if, before sentencing, he marries her.

The practice of seclusion

Seclusion of women known to be an accepted practice *early 2000*

Women are restricted in their public movements, and often strictly cloistered in the home. In many of these countries, seclusion is practiced only among some ethnic or religious groups.

TUNISIA
MOROCCO
IRAN
AFGHANISTAN
PAKISTAN
QATAR
UAE
SAUDI ARABIA
OMAN
INDIA
BANGLADESH
ERITREA
YEMEN
NIGER
especially among Hausa and Fulani
NIGERIA (primarily in the north)
CAMEROON (primarily in the north)

18 Copyright © Myriad Editions

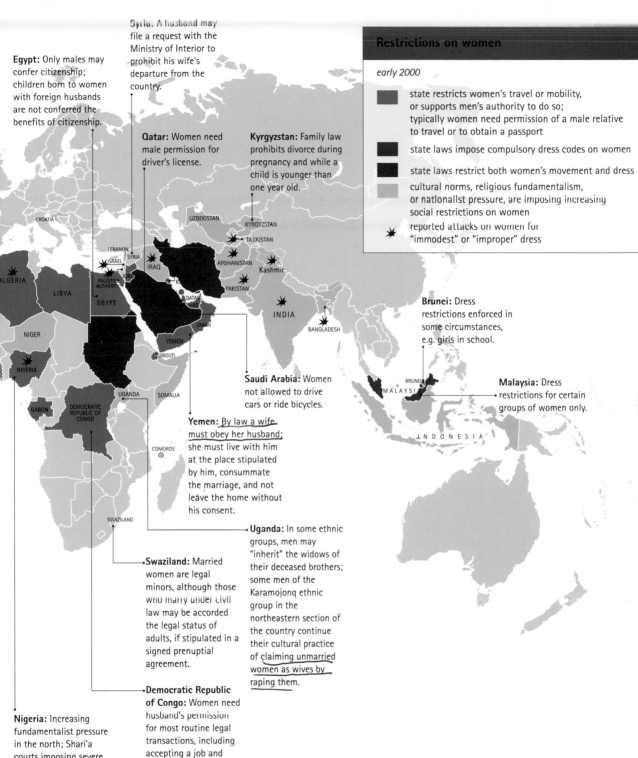

Egypt: Only males may confer citizenship; children born to women with foreign husbands are not conferred the benefits of citizenship.

Syria: A husband may file a request with the Ministry of Interior to prohibit his wife's departure from the country.

Qatar: Women need male permission for driver's license.

Kyrgyzstan: Family law prohibits divorce during pregnancy and while a child is younger than one year old.

CROATIA

UZBEKISTAN

KYRGYZSTAN

TAJIKISTAN

AFGHANISTAN

Kashmir

LEBANON
ISRAEL · SYRIA
PALESTINE
AUTHORITY · JORD
IRAQ

PAKISTAN

ALGERIA

LIBYA

EGYPT

QATAR
UAE

INDIA

NIGER

OMAN

BANGLADESH

YEMEN

DJIBOUTI

Brunei: Dress restrictions enforced in some circumstances, e.g. girls in school.

NIGERIA

GABON

DEMOCRATIC REPUBLIC OF CONGO

UGANDA

SOMALIA

SWAZILAND

BRUNEI
MALAYSIA

Malaysia: Dress restrictions for certain groups of women only.

INDONESIA

Saudi Arabia: Women not allowed to drive cars or ride bicycles.

COMOROS

Yemen: By law a wife must obey her husband; she must live with him at the place stipulated by him, consummate the marriage, and not leave the home without his consent.

Uganda: In some ethnic groups, men may "inherit" the widows of their deceased brothers; some men of the Karamojonq ethnic group in the northeastern section of the country continue their cultural practice of claiming unmarried women as wives by raping them.

Swaziland: Married women are legal minors, although those who marry under civil law may be accorded the legal status of adults, if stipulated in a signed prenuptial agreement.

Democratic Republic of Congo: Women need husband's permission for most routine legal transactions, including accepting a job and opening a bank account.

Nigeria: Increasing fundamentalist pressure in the north; Shari'a courts imposing severe sentences, including flogging and death by stoning, on women for sexual impropriety.

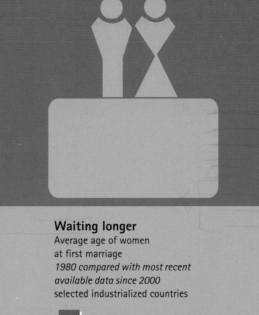

Waiting longer
Average age of women
at first marriage
*1980 compared with most recent
available data since 2000*
selected industrialized countries

 1980

 2000

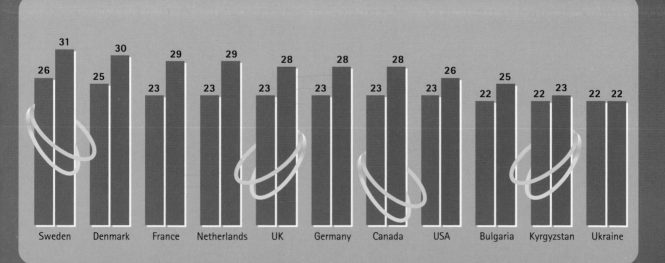

	Sweden	Denmark	France	Netherlands	UK	Germany	Canada	USA	Bulgaria	Kyrgyzstan	Ukraine
1980	26	25	23	23	23	23	23	23	22	22	22
2000	31	30	29	29	28	28	28	26	25	23	22

4 Households

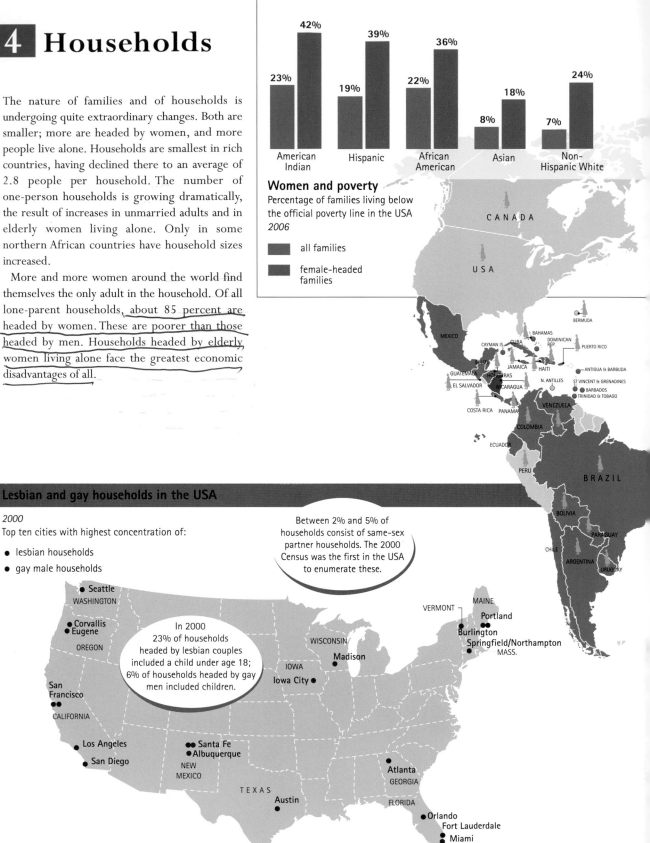

The nature of families and of households is undergoing quite extraordinary changes. Both are smaller; more are headed by women, and more people live alone. Households are smallest in rich countries, having declined there to an average of 2.8 people per household. The number of one-person households is growing dramatically, the result of increases in unmarried adults and in elderly women living alone. Only in some northern African countries have household sizes increased.

More and more women around the world find themselves the only adult in the household. Of all lone-parent households, about 85 percent are headed by women. These are poorer than those headed by men. Households headed by elderly women living alone face the greatest economic disadvantages of all.

Women and poverty

Percentage of families living below the official poverty line in the USA
2006

- all families
- female-headed families

	American Indian	Hispanic	African American	Asian	Non-Hispanic White
all families	23%	19%	22%	8%	7%
female-headed families	42%	39%	36%	18%	24%

Lesbian and gay households in the USA

2000
Top ten cities with highest concentration of:

- lesbian households
- gay male households

Between 2% and 5% of households consist of same-sex partner households. The 2000 Census was the first in the USA to enumerate these.

In 2000 23% of households headed by lesbian couples included a child under age 18; 6% of households headed by gay men included children.

Seattle — WASHINGTON
Corvallis — Eugene — OREGON
San Francisco — CALIFORNIA
Los Angeles
San Diego
Santa Fe — Albuquerque — NEW MEXICO
TEXAS
Austin
WISCONSIN — Madison
IOWA — Iowa City
Atlanta — GEORGIA
FLORIDA
Orlando
Fort Lauderdale
Miami
VERMONT — MAINE — Portland
Burlington
Springfield/Northampton — MASS.

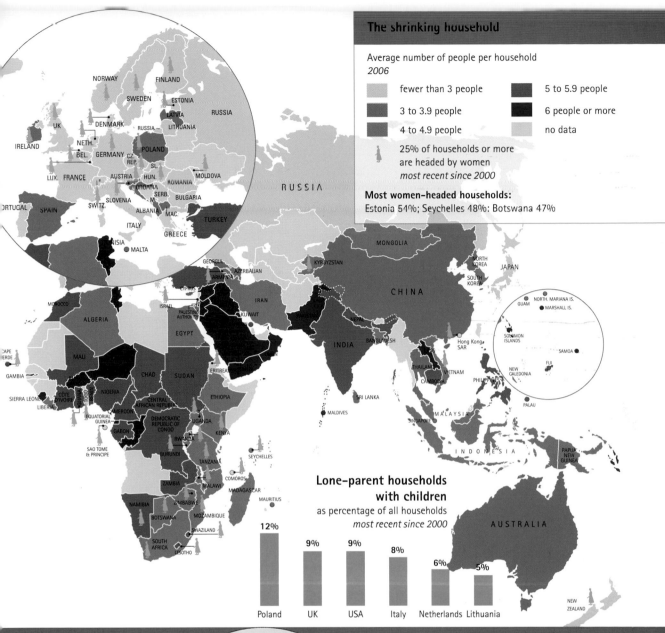

The shrinking household

Average number of people per household
2006

- fewer than 3 people
- 3 to 3.9 people
- 4 to 4.9 people
- 5 to 5.9 people
- 6 people or more
- no data

25% of households or more
are headed by women
most recent since 2000

Most women–headed households:
Estonia 54%; Seychelles 48%; Botswana 47%

Lone-parent households
with children
as percentage of all households
most recent since 2000

Poland	UK	USA	Italy	Netherlands	Lithuania
12%	9%	9%	8%	6%	5%

Living alone

One-person households
as % of all households
most recent since 2000

- 30% or more
- 20% – 29%
- fewer than 20%

women comprise more
than 60% of one-person
households *most recent
since 2000*

23

5 Marriage and Divorce

With the exception of the Caribbean region, which is notable for its relatively low rates of marriage, most women and men in the world spend most of their lives married. However, the nature of marriage varies widely from place to place, and between men and women.

Worldwide, women marry younger than men. In some places the gap is extreme. For example, in Niger, 70 percent of girls, but only 4 percent of boys are married by age 19; in Honduras, the figure is 30 percent of girls and 7 percent of boys.

The idea that married women "belong" to their husbands still dominates gender relations in most countries, and is often backed up by law. In some countries women need their husband's permission to buy or sell property, to have an abortion, to travel outside the country (see Map 3), or to take up employment. In some places, widows can even be "inherited" along with other possessions. The notion that women are the "property" of their husbands is a potent ideological prop of domestic violence (see Map 7).

Marriage is changing. Polygamy is being challenged in many of the countries where it is practiced. In most industrialized countries, the women are marrying later, and more women are not getting married, or cohabiting before marriage. Legal recognition for gay unions expands the boundaries of marriage (see Map 6).

Worldwide almost 90% of adults are married for at least some portion of their lives.

The highest rates of girl-child marriage are found in Bangladesh, CAR, Chad, Guinea, Mali, and Niger. In these countries, more than 60% of girls aged under 18 are married.

Polygamous marriages take place in significant numbers elsewhere, including in Algeria, Bahrain, Bangladesh, Jordan, India, Iran, Iraq, Lebanon, Nepal, Oman, Pakistan, Syrian Arab Republic, United Arab Emirates, and Yemen.

Polygamy in Africa

Percentage of women aged 15–49
married to men who have more than one wife
2000 or latest available data

- 50% or more
- 40% – 49%
- 30% – 39%
- 20% – 29%
- 10% – 19%
- fewer than 10%
- other countries

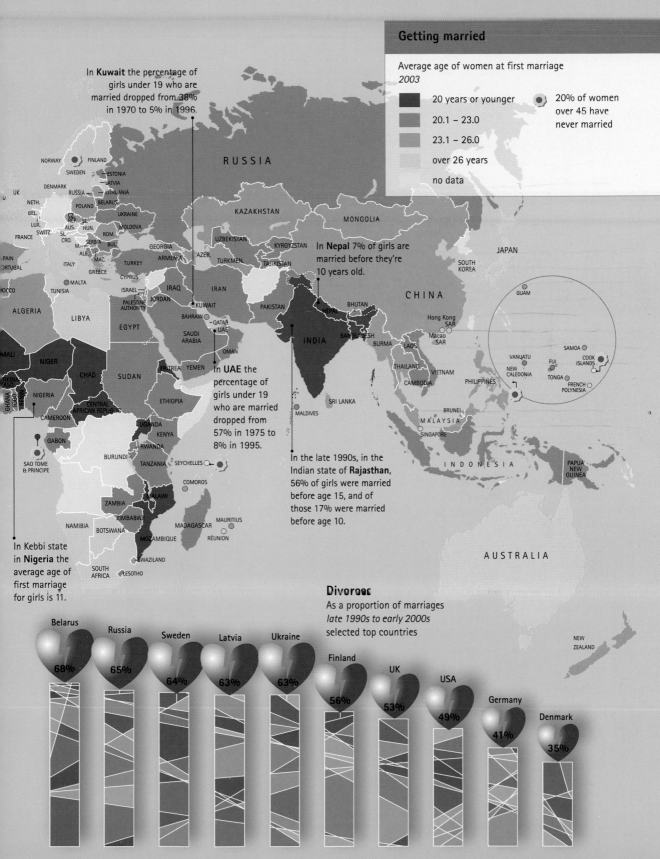

Getting married

Average age of women at first marriage
2003

- 20 years or younger
- 20.1 – 23.0
- 23.1 – 26.0
- over 26 years
- no data

20% of women over 45 have never married

In **Kuwait** the percentage of girls under 19 who are married dropped from 38% in 1970 to 5% in 1996.

In **Nepal** 7% of girls are married before they're 10 years old.

In **UAE** the percentage of girls under 19 who are married dropped from 57% in 1975 to 8% in 1995.

In the late 1990s, in the Indian state of **Rajasthan**, 56% of girls were married before age 15, and of those 17% were married before age 10.

In Kebbi state in **Nigeria** the average age of first marriage for girls is 11.

Divorce

As a proportion of marriages
late 1990s to early 2000s
selected top countries

- Belarus 68%
- Russia 65%
- Sweden 64%
- Latvia 63%
- Ukraine 63%
- Finland 56%
- UK 53%
- USA 49%
- Germany 41%
- Denmark 35%

25

6 Lesbian Rights

Lesbians and gay men are increasingly visible in many countries. Lesbian and gay organizing over the past decade has been impressive. In some countries, governments are slowly responding to pressure to offer protection and recognition for lesbian and gay rights.

In other places, though, hatred of homosexuals is institutionalized and encouraged, and repression of lesbians and gay men remains severe. Lesbians are often raped, sometimes by family members, as a punishment or as a "treatment" for their homosexuality. While it is difficult to generalize about what provokes such strong homophobia, it is clear that the presence of lesbians and gay men challenges complacency about narrow definitions of what constitutes a family, a household, or "normal" sexual relationships.

When women step outside of heterosexual norms, they are seen as being doubly subversive — both as members of a sexual minority, and also as women who are rejecting male authority.

World Health Organization 1991 removes homosexuality from its classification list of diseases.

USA 2003
A Supreme Court ruling invalidated all remaining state-level sodomy laws; these laws had been used primarily to police gay men and lesbians.

Ecuador 1998
The first Latin American country to include sexual orientation rights and protection in their national constitution.

Chile 1998
Criminalization of same-sex sexual relationships repealed.

Where homosexuality is criminalized, the prevailing assumption is that recognition of same-sex relationships is also not possible.

Same-sex partnership recognition

Status as of mid-2008

- same-sex marriages and partnerships accorded the same legal standing as heterosexual marriages in national law
- same-sex partnerships have similar status to heterosexual marriages
- same-sex partnerships have legal standing under national law, but not on parity with heterosexual marriages
- legal recognition of same-sex partnerships is extended at some state or local levels
- national-level legislation bans federal recognition of same-sex partnerships

USA
Federal ban on same sex marriages/unions, but some local recognition.

Vietnam
Same-sex marriage banned since 1998.

Uganda
Constitution amended in 2005 to ban same-sex marriage.

Australia
Federal ban on same-sex marriage, but some local recognition of partnerships.

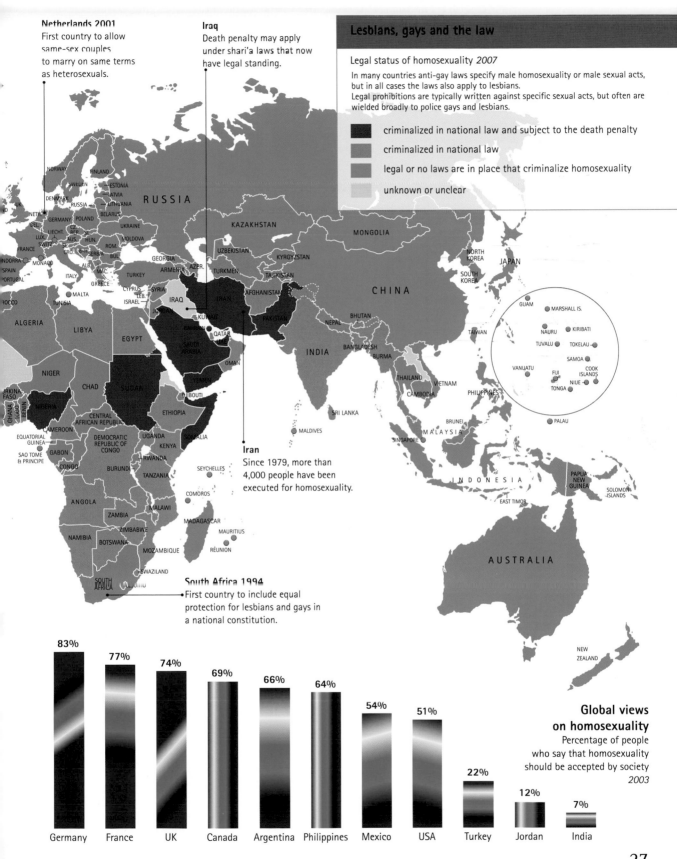

Netherlands 2001
First country to allow same-sex couples to marry on same terms as heterosexuals.

Iraq
Death penalty may apply under shari'a laws that now have legal standing.

Legal status of homosexuality *2007*

In many countries anti-gay laws specify male homosexuality or male sexual acts, but in all cases the laws also apply to lesbians.
Legal prohibitions are typically written against specific sexual acts, but often are wielded broadly to police gays and lesbians.

- criminalized in national law and subject to the death penalty
- criminalized in national law
- legal or no laws are in place that criminalize homosexuality
- unknown or unclear

Iran
Since 1979, more than 4,000 people have been executed for homosexuality.

South Africa 1994
First country to include equal protection for lesbians and gays in a national constitution.

83%	Germany
77%	France
74%	UK
69%	Canada
66%	Argentina
64%	Philippines
54%	Mexico
51%	USA
22%	Turkey
12%	Jordan
7%	India

Global views on homosexuality
Percentage of people who say that homosexuality should be accepted by society
2003

Domestic Violence

For millions of women, the home is the most dangerous place they could be. Far from being a place of safety, the family is often a cradle of violence. Women suffer cruelties in their homes every day, from all family members. Domestic violence is a means of keeping women "in their place," literally confined to relationship, household, or family structures defined by patriarchal authority. Violence against women sustains particular sexual, family, and household structures, and keeps women subordinate to them.

Domestic violence is the most ubiquitous constant in women's lives around the world. There is virtually no place where it is not a significant problem, and women of no race, class, or age are exempt from its reach. Statistics on domestic violence are notoriously unreliable. What information we do have about it is only available because of concerted campaigns by women to bring attention to this issue.

Violence against women is often ignored or even condoned by the state on the grounds that it is a "private" matter.

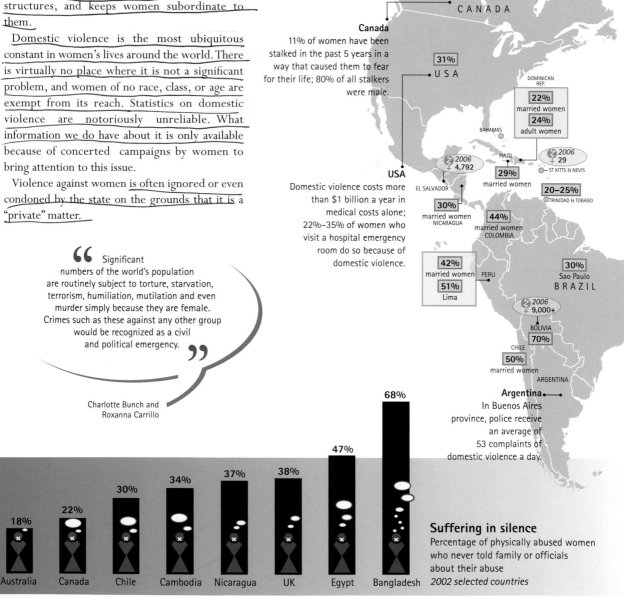

When women say it's OK
Percentage of women who say it is acceptable for a husband to beat his wife for one or more specific reasons – burning food, arguing with him, going out without telling him, neglecting the children, refusing sex
2004 selected countries

- Egypt 94%
- Zambia 91%
- India 70%
- Ethiopia 69%
- Haiti 48%
- Cambodia 46%
- Nicaragua 34%

> **Significant** numbers of the world's population are routinely subject to torture, starvation, terrorism, humiliation, mutilation and even murder simply because they are female. Crimes such as these against any other group would be recognized as a civil and political emergency.
>
> Charlotte Bunch and Roxanna Carrillo

Canada
11% of women have been stalked in the past 5 years in a way that caused them to fear for their life; 80% of all stalkers were male.

CANADA

Canada

31%
USA

USA
Domestic violence costs more than $1 billion a year in medical costs alone; 22%–35% of women who visit a hospital emergency room do so because of domestic violence.

BAHAMAS

DOMINICAN REP.
22% married women
24% adult women

2006 ⚡ 4,792

HAITI
29% married women

ST KITTS & NEVIS

2006 ⚡ 29

20–25%
TRINIDAD & TOBAGO

EL SALVADOR
30% married women
NICARAGUA

44% married women
COLOMBIA

42% married women PERU
51% Lima

30% Sao Paulo
BRAZIL

2006 ⚡ 9,000+
BOLIVIA
70%

CHILE
50% married women

ARGENTINA

Argentina
In Buenos Aires province, police receive an average of 53 complaints of domestic violence a day.

Suffering in silence
Percentage of physically abused women who never told family or officials about their abuse
2002 selected countries

- Australia 18%
- Canada 22%
- Chile 30%
- Cambodia 34%
- Nicaragua 37%
- UK 38%
- Egypt 47%
- Bangladesh 68%

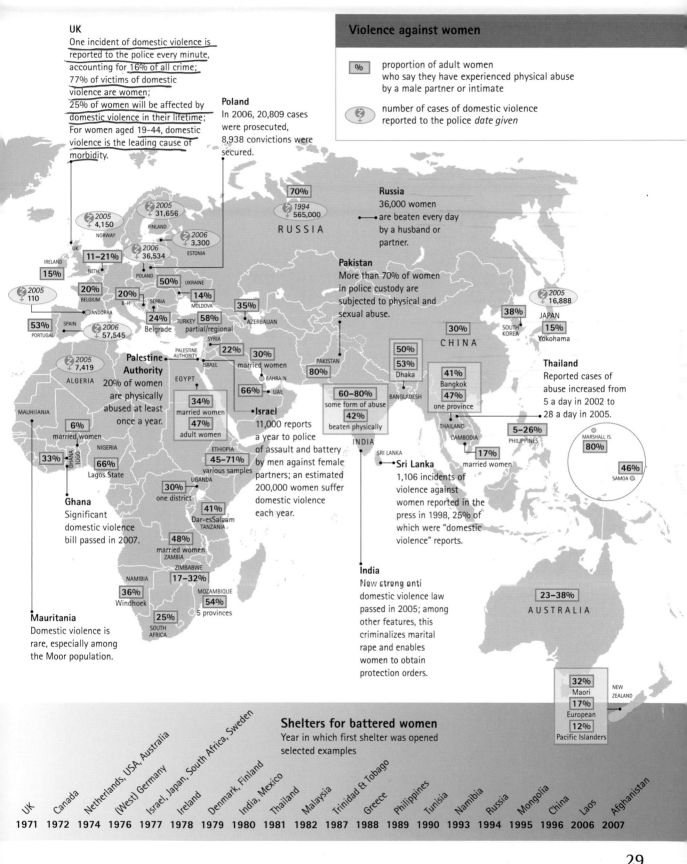

Violence against women

% proportion of adult women who say they have experienced physical abuse by a male partner or intimate

⚡ number of cases of domestic violence reported to the police *date given*

UK
One incident of domestic violence is reported to the police every minute, accounting for 16% of all crime; 77% of victims of domestic violence are women; 25% of women will be affected by domestic violence in their lifetime; For women aged 19–44, domestic violence is the leading cause of morbidity.

Poland
In 2006, 20,809 cases were prosecuted, 8,938 convictions were secured.

Russia
36,000 women are beaten every day by a husband or partner.

Pakistan
More than 70% of women in police custody are subjected to physical and sexual abuse.

Thailand
Reported cases of abuse increased from 5 a day in 2002 to 28 a day in 2005.

Palestine Authority
20% of women are physically abused at least once a year.

Israel
11,000 reports a year to police of assault and battery by men against female partners; an estimated 200,000 women suffer domestic violence each year.

Sri Lanka
1,106 incidents of violence against women reported in the press in 1998, 25% of which were "domestic violence" reports.

India
New strong anti domestic violence law passed in 2005; among other features, this criminalizes marital rape and enables women to obtain protection orders.

Ghana
Significant domestic violence bill passed in 2007.

Mauritania
Domestic violence is rare, especially among the Moor population.

⚡ 2005 4,150 NORWAY
⚡ 2005 31,656 FINLAND
⚡ 2006 3,300 ESTONIA
⚡ 2006 36,534 POLAND
⚡ 1994 565,000 RUSSIA
70%
⚡ 2005 16,888 JAPAN
UK 11–21%
IRELAND 15%
⚡ 2005 110 BELGIUM
NETH.
20% B-H
20% BELGIUM
50% POLAND
14% MOLDOVA
35% AZERBAIJAN
38% SOUTH KOREA
15% Yokohama
⚡ 2006 57,545 SPAIN
53% PORTUGAL
⚡ 2005 7,419 ALGERIA
ANDORRA
24% Belgrade SERBIA
58% TURKEY partial/regional
22% SYRIA
30% married women
66% UAE
BAHRAIN
ISRAEL
PALESTINE AUTHORITY
30% PAKISTAN
80%
50% CHINA
53% Dhaka
60–80% some form of abuse BANGLADESH
42% beaten physically INDIA
41% Bangkok THAILAND
47% one province
5–26% PHILIPPINES
17% married women CAMBODIA
80% MARSHALL IS.
46% SAMOA
EGYPT
34% married women
47% adult women
6% married women MAURITANIA
33% GHANA TOGO
66% Lagos State NIGERIA
45–71% various samples ETHIOPIA
30% one district UGANDA
41% Dar-esSalaam TANZANIA
48% married women ZAMBIA
17–32% ZIMBABWE
36% Windhoek NAMIBIA
54% 5 provinces MOZAMBIQUE
25% SOUTH AFRICA
SRI LANKA
23–38% AUSTRALIA
32% Maori
17% European
12% Pacific Islanders NEW ZEALAND

Shelters for battered women
Year in which first shelter was opened selected examples

UK	Canada	Netherlands, USA, Australia	(West) Germany	Israel, Japan, South Africa, Sweden	Ireland	Denmark, Finland	India, Mexico	Thailand	Malaysia	Trinidad & Tobago	Greece	Philippines	Tunisia	Namibia	Russia	Mongolia	China	Laos	Afghanistan
1971	1972	1974	1976	1977	1978	1979	1980	1981	1982	1987	1988	1989	1990	1993	1994	1995	1996	2006	2007

29

At least one woman in three in the world has been beaten, coerced into sex, or otherwise abused in her lifetime by a member of her family. For the majority of such women, the abuse is repeated over months or years. In an astonishing number of cases, "ordinary" domestic violence culminates in murder. Violence against women often escalates when the woman tries to leave an abusive relationship – this is when violent partners are most likely to turn to murder.

Some patterns of women-murder are culture and place-specific: dowry-burnings in India and Pakistan, bride-price murders in Zambia, gun-murders in the USA. "Honor killing" is a term used to identify a form of legally or socially sanctioned revenge exercised within a family against a woman who is deemed to have soiled the family's honor, usually through behavior that is judged to be sexually inappropriate. Women's human rights activists are increasing pressure on governments to take action against honor killings, but many governments are reluctant to do so.

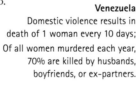

Canada
40%–70% of all female murder victims are killed by their husbands or boyfriends. In 2003, 78 people were killed by their spouse; 64 of these victims were women.
1994–2003: 1,695 "family-related" homicides.

USA
On average, 23 women a week are killed by intimates; this has held steady for more than a decade.
Of all women murdered between 1976–2005, 42% were killed by an intimate or other family member;
74% of all murders of women from domestic violence occur *after* the woman has left the relationship, filed for divorce or sought a restraining order against her partner.

Mexico
In Cuidad Juarez and Chihuahua more than 500 women have been murdered since 1993, and dozens more are missing.

Guatemala
More than 2,400 women were murdered between 2000–06; 97% of cases are unsolved.

Jamaica
90 women a year are killed by domestic violence.

Dominican Republic
In the first 6 months of 2006, 43 women were killed by partners or former partners.

El Salvador
In the first 8 months of 2006, 286 women were killed.

Venezuela
Domestic violence results in death of 1 woman every 10 days;
Of all women murdered each year, 70% are killed by husbands, boyfriends, or ex-partners.

Colombia
A woman is reportedly killed by her partner or ex-partner every 6 days.

Brazil
72% of murdered women were killed by a relative or friend.

Uruguay
Domestic violence results in death of 1 woman every 9 days.

Homicide in the USA

Murder as a percentage of all deaths by age group *2001*
- male
- female

African American

	15–19	20–24 years old	25–34
male	45	46	27
female	22	17	11

White American

	15–19	20–24 years old	25–34
male	10	10	7
female	6	9	5

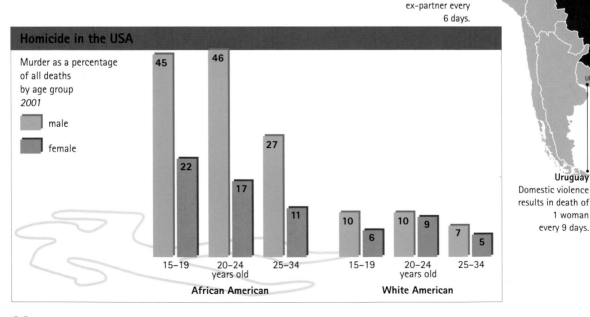

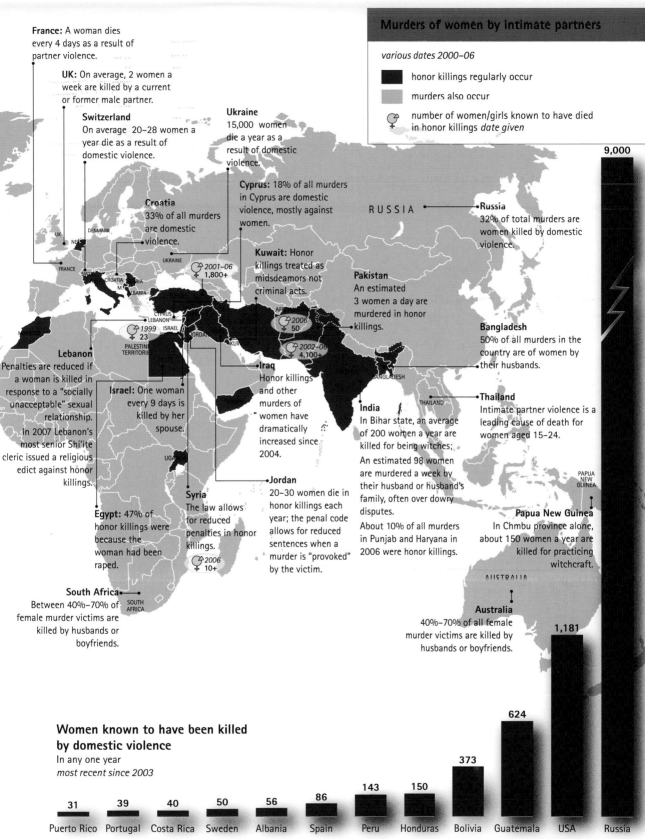

France: A woman dies every 4 days as a result of partner violence.

UK: On average, 2 women a week are killed by a current or former male partner.

Switzerland On average 20–28 women a year die as a result of domestic violence.

Ukraine 15,000 women die a year as a result of domestic violence.

Cyprus: 18% of all murders in Cyprus are domestic violence, mostly against women.

Croatia 33% of all murders are domestic violence.

Kuwait: Honor killings treated as midsdeamors not criminal acts.

Russia 32% of total murders are women killed by domestic violence.

Pakistan An estimated 3 women a day are murdered in honor killings.

Bangladesh 50% of all murders in the country are of women by their husbands.

Lebanon Penalties are reduced if a woman is killed in response to a "socially unacceptable" sexual relationship.
In 2007 Lebanon's most senior Shi'ite cleric issued a religious edict against honor killings.

Israel: One woman every 9 days is killed by her spouse.

Iraq Honor killings and other murders of women have dramatically increased since 2004.

India In Bihar state, an average of 200 women a year are killed for being witches;
An estimated 98 women are murdered a week by their husband or husband's family, often over dowry disputes.
About 10% of all murders in Punjab and Haryana in 2006 were honor killings.

Thailand Intimate partner violence is a leading cause of death for women aged 15–24.

Egypt: 47% of honor killings were because the woman had been raped.

Syria The law allows for reduced penalties in honor killings.

Jordan 20–30 women die in honor killings each year; the penal code allows for reduced sentences when a murder is "provoked" by the victim.

Papua New Guinea In Chmbu province alone, about 150 women a year are killed for practicing witchcraft.

South Africa Between 40%–70% of female murder victims are killed by husbands or boyfriends.

Australia 40%–70% of all female murder victims are killed by husbands or boyfriends.

Murders of women by intimate partners

various dates 2000–06

- ■ honor killings regularly occur
- ▧ murders also occur
- ⚧ number of women/girls known to have died in honor killings *date given*

2001–06 1,800+

1999 23

2006 50

2002–06 4,100+

2006 10+

Women known to have been killed by domestic violence
In any one year
most recent since 2003

Puerto Rico	Portugal	Costa Rica	Sweden	Albania	Spain	Peru	Honduras	Bolivia	Guatemala	USA	Russia
31	39	40	50	56	86	143	150	373	624	1,181	9,000

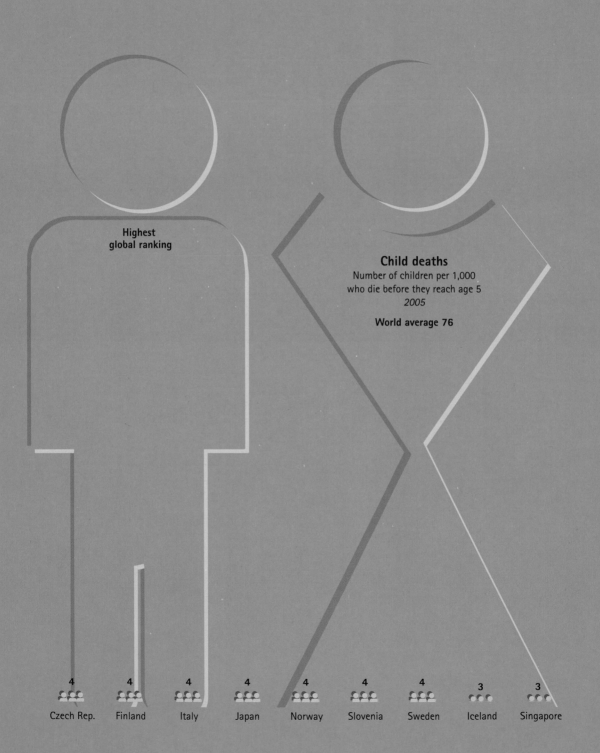

Highest
global ranking

Child deaths
Number of children per 1,000
who die before they reach age 5
2005

World average 76

4	4	4	4	4	4	4	3	3
Czech Rep.	Finland	Italy	Japan	Norway	Slovenia	Sweden	Iceland	Singapore

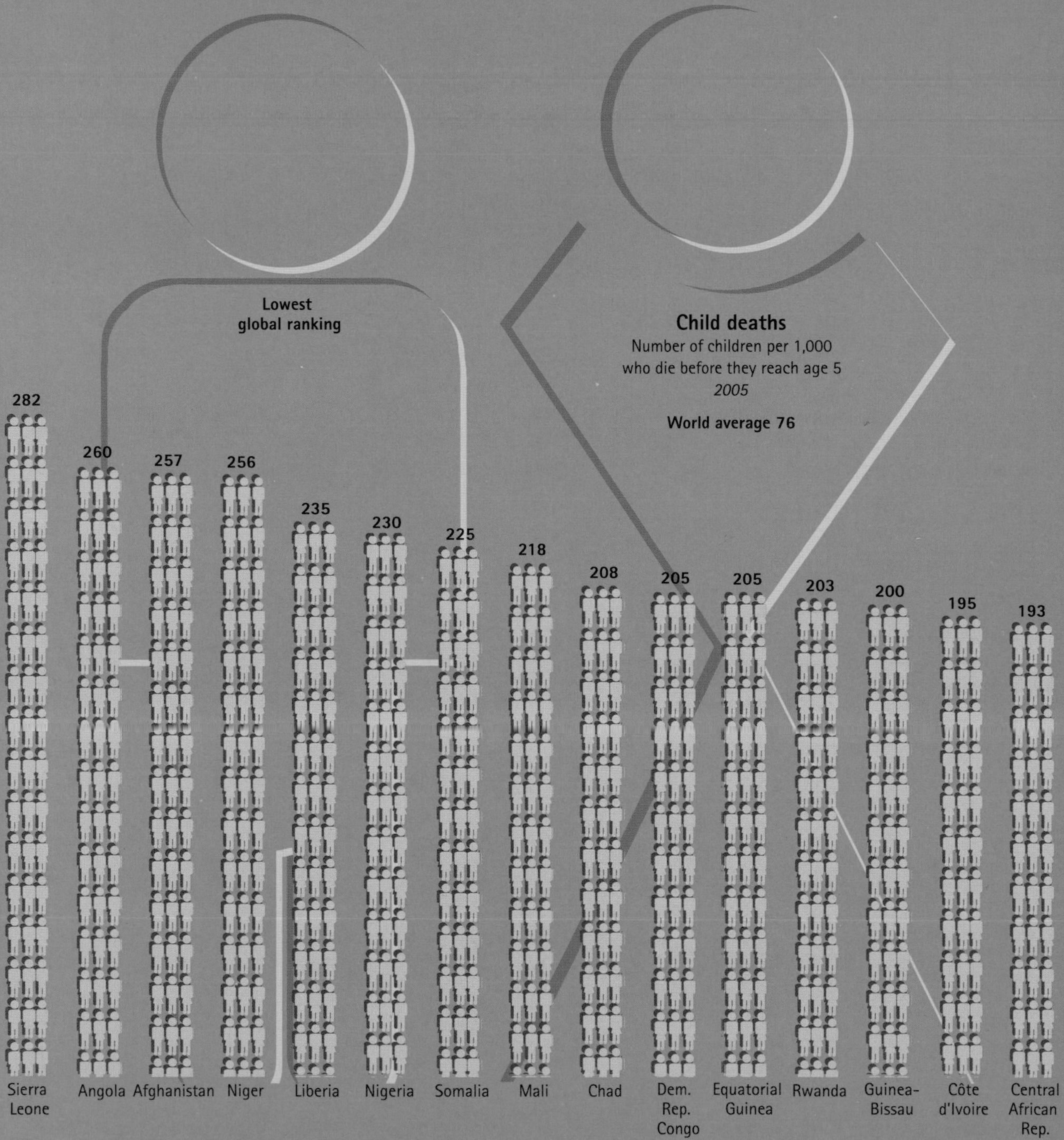

**Lowest
global ranking**

Child deaths
Number of children per 1,000
who die before they reach age 5
2005

World average 76

282
Sierra Leone

260
Angola

257
Afghanistan

256
Niger

235
Liberia

230
Nigeria

225
Somalia

218
Mali

208
Chad

205
Dem. Rep. Congo

205
Equatorial Guinea

203
Rwanda

200
Guinea-Bissau

195
Côte d'Ivoire

193
Central African Rep.

In many countries, women are engaged in childbearing for most of their adult lives. Nonetheless, on worldwide average, women are having fewer children than did their mothers and grandmothers. This trend reflects two main factors: the increasing availability of reproductive health services – including the liberalization of abortion laws (Map 11) – and incremental improvements in women's status and autonomy.

Sexual politics strongly influence the number of children women have or want to have. Almost everywhere, notions of what constitutes "normal" masculinity and femininity are defined in reference to fertility and family. It is common for both men's and women's social status to be pegged to the number of children they produce. Fertility rates are also shaped by marriage norms (Map 5), the prevalence of polygamy, son preference (Map 13), and presumptions about the sexual "needs" of men and women. Most surveys show that women typically want fewer children than do their male partners; thus, the gendered balance of power within the household is important in determining family size.

Government health, economic, and social security policies further shape family-size decisions; in much of the world, large families provide economic security and provide the primary social safety net. Additionally, national and international government population policies strongly influence fertility norms.

Women want fewer children

The number of children that women say makes the ideal family size changes over time
early 1980s compared with mid-2000s
selected countries

■ 1980s   ■ 2000s

Country	1980s	2000s
Nigeria	8.3	6.7
Kenya	6.8	3.9
Morocco	4.9	2.9
Philippines	4.4	3.0
Indonesia	4.1	2.9
Colombia	3.5	2.2

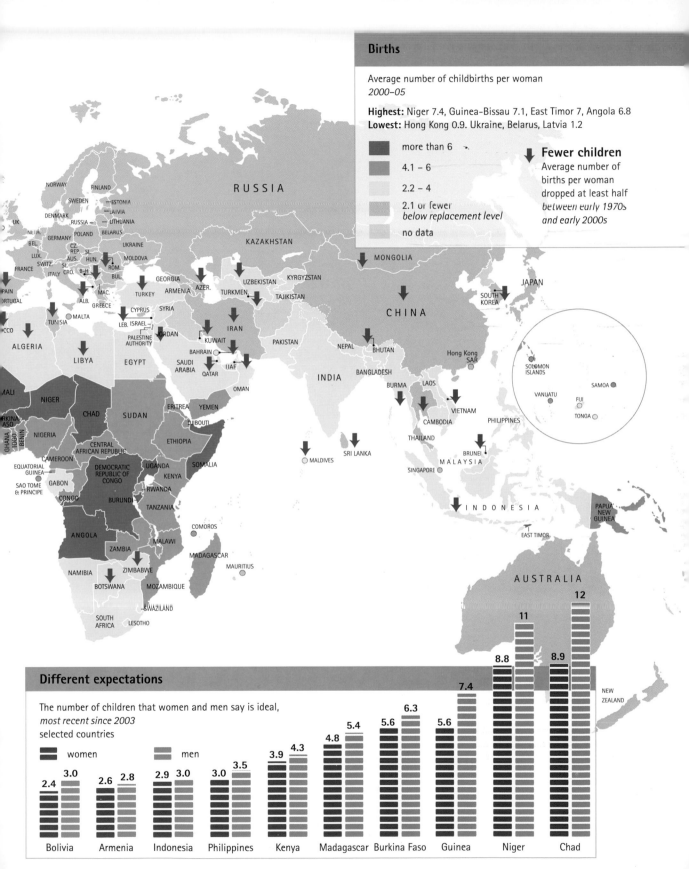

Births

Average number of childbirths per woman
2000–05

Highest: Niger 7.4, Guinea-Bissau 7.1, East Timor 7, Angola 6.8
Lowest: Hong Kong 0.9, Ukraine, Belarus, Latvia 1.2

- more than 6
- 4.1 – 6
- 2.2 – 4
- 2.1 or fewer
  below replacement level
- no data

Fewer children
Average number of births per woman dropped at least half *between early 1970s and early 2000s*

Different expectations

The number of children that women and men say is ideal,
most recent since 2003
selected countries

- women
- men

Country	women	men
Bolivia	2.4	3.0
Armenia	2.6	2.8
Indonesia	2.9	3.0
Philippines	3.0	3.5
Kenya	3.9	4.3
Madagascar	4.8	5.4
Burkina Faso	5.6	6.3
Guinea	5.6	7.4
Niger	8.8	11
Chad	8.9	12

35

10 | Contraception

Since the 1970s, women's use of contraceptives has increased dramatically, and more than 50 percent of the world's women now use modern contraceptive methods. Access to reliable contraceptives is a powerful force in advancing women's liberation and autonomy.

Use of contraceptives remains uneven. Women in wealthy countries and urban areas generally have the best access to contraceptive services. Unmet need among the world's women is great and hundreds of millions of women do not have access to contraceptives. Millions more are dependent on foreign aid donors for their supply. Female sterilization remains the most common contraceptive method.

The politics of contraceptives development and distribution are complex and troubling. Abuses are common. In the past few decades, governments of several countries, including China, India, and the USA, have imposed programs of forced sterilization on minority or poor women. Global pharmaceutical companies have aggressively marketed unsafe or experimental contraceptives to poor women. Women still face the dilemma that the safest contraceptives are not the most effective, while the most effective are not necessarily the safest.

Unmet need
2007

■ 20% or more of married women would like to limit childbearing but do not use any contraceptive device or technique

other
5%

condoms
7%

male sterilization
8%

traditional
methods
10%

the Pill
11%

IUD
25%

female
sterilization
34%

Types of contraception
Proportion of married or "in union"
women worldwide using each method
late 1990s or latest available data

CANADA — 21

USA — 23

MEXICO — 31

DOMINICAN REP. — 41

CUBA
JAMAICA   HAITI
PUERTO RICO — 46
TRINIDAD & TOBAGO

GUATEMALA   HONDURAS
EL SALVADOR — 32   NICARAGUA — 26
COSTA RICA — 21
COLOMBIA — 27
ECUADOR — 23
PERU — 40

BRAZIL

BOLIVIA

PARAGUAY

Emergency contraception

■ emergency contraception available *2007*

■ emergency contraception available only with prescription

□ no data

"Emergency contraception" (EC) prevents pregnancy after intercourse has occurred. EC methods include special doses of birth control pills or insertion of an IUD. EC can be used up to three days after intercourse, and offers protection for women who have been raped, experienced contraceptive failure, or engaged in unprotected sex. RU486 (Mifepristone) is a drug that produces a miscarriage in the first weeks of pregnancy. Because it is a non-surgical abortifacient, RU 486 has been particularly controversial.

36   Copyright © Myriad Editions

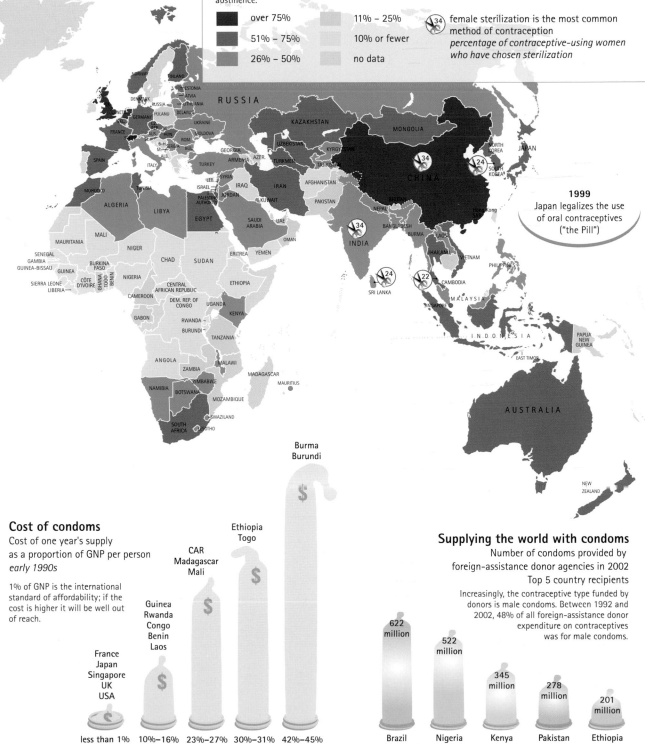

Use of contraception

Proportion of married women using "modern" contraception *most recent since 2000*

"**Modern**" contraceptive methods include oral contraceptives, IUD, injectibles, sterilization.
"**Traditional**" contraceptive methods include folk remedies, herbal remedies, rhythm, withdrawal, planned abstinence.

- over 75%
- 51% – 75%
- 26% – 50%
- 11% – 25%
- 10% or fewer
- no data

(34) female sterilization is the most common method of contraception
percentage of contraceptive-using women who have chosen sterilization

1999
Japan legalizes the use of oral contraceptives ("the Pill")

Cost of condoms

Cost of one year's supply as a proportion of GNP per person
early 1990s

1% of GNP is the international standard of affordability; if the cost is higher it will be well out of reach.

France Japan Singapore UK USA	Guinea Rwanda Congo Benin Laos	CAR Madagascar Mali	Ethiopia Togo	Burma Burundi
less than 1%	10%–16%	23%–27%	30%–31%	42%–45%

Supplying the world with condoms

Number of condoms provided by foreign-assistance donor agencies in 2002
Top 5 country recipients

Increasingly, the contraceptive type funded by donors is male condoms. Between 1992 and 2002, 48% of all foreign-assistance donor expenditure on contraceptives was for male condoms.

Brazil	Nigeria	Kenya	Pakistan	Ethiopia
622 million	522 million	345 million	278 million	201 million

37

11 Abortion

There are an estimated 25 million to 30 million legal abortions worldwide each year, and a further 20 million unsafe, illegal abortions. Most women in the world who seek abortions are married, or live in stable unions, and already have children.

The struggle over abortion rights is at its heart a struggle about women's autonomy. The extent to which women control their reproductive choices affects their freedom in all other spheres: their participation in the economy, education, the household, and in political and civic arenas, as well as their degree of economic and social autonomy from men.

The legal status of abortion does not fully reflect the reality of abortion availability. In countries where abortions are legal, it does not necessarily mean they are available. Myriad factors affect women's actual access to abortion services, including their class, race, age, and geographic location. In some countries where abortion is legal, government support for it is nonetheless weak, and governments can and do undercut the availability of abortion services.

Still, the legal context of abortion is critically important. Restrictive legislation compels women to choose between unsafe abortions or unwanted births. Millions of women each year are desperate enough to seek clandestine abortions; tens of thousands die as a result. Even the most restrictive abortion laws typically allow some exceptions – for example, when pregnancy threatens the woman's life – but a surprising number of governments do not allow abortions even when the pregnancy is the result of rape or incest.

Since the 1980s, the worldwide trend has been towards more liberal abortion laws – almost entirely due to persistent feminist activism. Nonetheless, about one- quarter of the world's women still live in countries with highly restrictive abortion laws.

In 2001, President George W. Bush banned foreign non-governmental organizations (NGOs) that receive USAID family planning funds from using any money (even their own, non-US money) to provide legal abortion services, lobby their own governments for abortion law reform, or even provide accurate medical counseling to women about abortion or referrals regarding abortion.

Anti-abortion backlash
USA and Canada *1997–2007*
• 2 abortion clinic workers murdered • 4 attempted murders
• 117 death threats • 181 stalking incidents against workers or patients • 43 arsons or bombings of clinics; 26 attempts
• 656 anthrax mail threats received.

In 2005, 87% of US counties were not served by an abortion provider.

Legal abortion
Number per 1,000 women aged 15–44
most recent since 2003
selected countries

Country	Number
India	3
Germany	8
Bahrain	11
Japan	12
Israel	14
Denmark	14
Canada	15
UK	17
France	17
Sweden	20
USA	21
China	24
Estonia	33
Russia	54

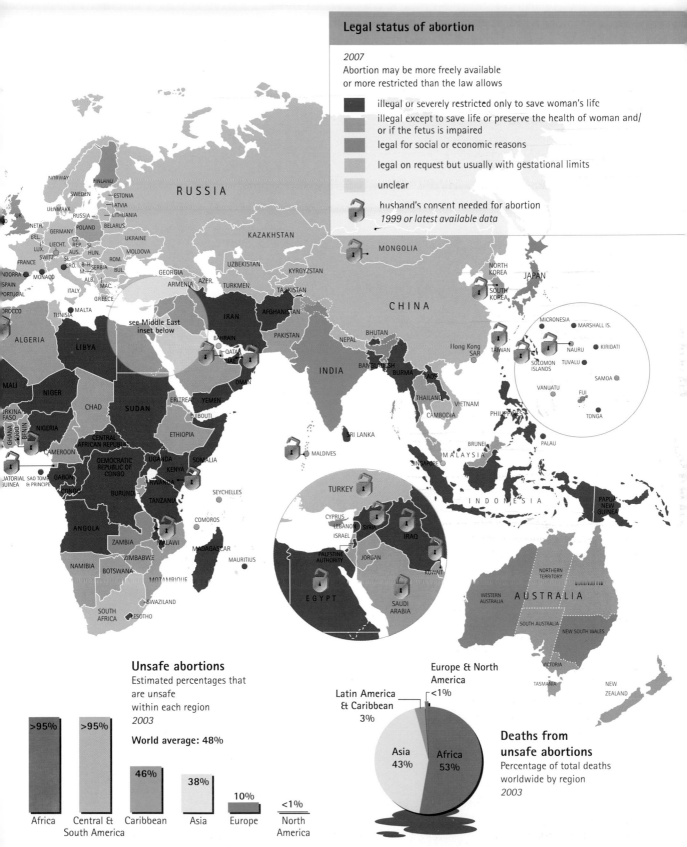

Legal status of abortion

see Middle East inset below

Unsafe abortions

Estimated percentages that
are unsafe
within each region
2003

World average: 48%

Africa	Central & South America	Caribbean	Asia	Europe	North America
>95%	>95%	46%	38%	10%	<1%

Deaths from unsafe abortions

Percentage of total deaths
worldwide by region
2003

- Europe & North America <1%
- Latin America & Caribbean 3%
- Asia 43%
- Africa 53%

Each year, about 200 million women become pregnant. Over half a million of these, will die as a result. Another 50 million women will suffer long-term disability or illness as a consequence of pregnancy and childbirth.

Of all the health measures monitored by the World Health Organization, the largest discrepancy between rich and poor countries occurs in maternal mortality. Most of these deaths could be prevented: by providing basic prenatal health care, improving maternal nutrition, and by providing the legal, social, and health support that would allow women to avoid unwanted pregnancies.

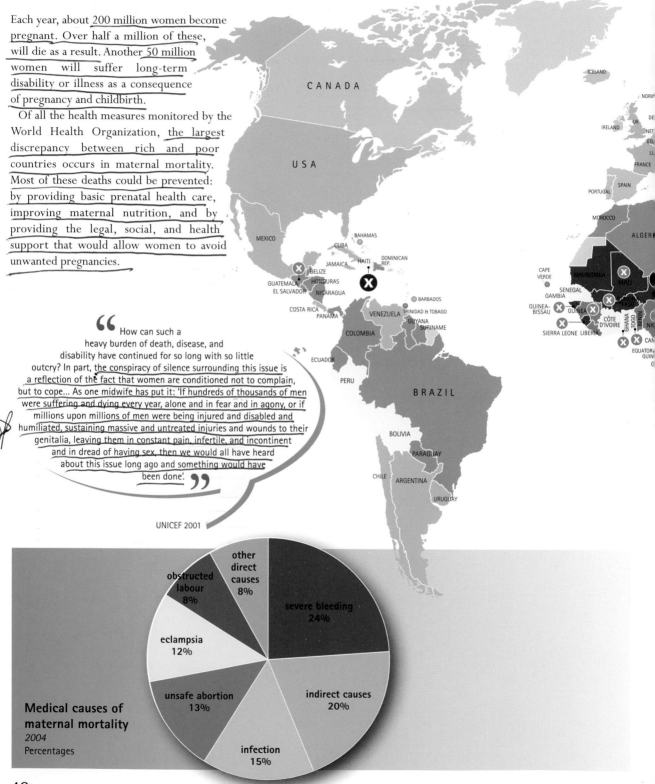

" How can such a heavy burden of death, disease, and disability have continued for so long with so little outcry? In part, the conspiracy of silence surrounding this issue is a reflection of the fact that women are conditioned not to complain, but to cope... As one midwife has put it: 'If hundreds of thousands of men were suffering and dying every year, alone and in fear and in agony, or if millions upon millions of men were being injured and disabled and humiliated, sustaining massive and untreated injuries and wounds to their genitalia, leaving them in constant pain, infertile, and incontinent and in dread of having sex, then we would all have heard about this issue long ago and something would have been done'. "

UNICEF 2001

Medical causes of maternal mortality
2004
Percentages

- severe bleeding 24%
- indirect causes 20%
- infection 15%
- unsafe abortion 13%
- eclampsia 12%
- obstructed labour 8%
- other direct causes 8%

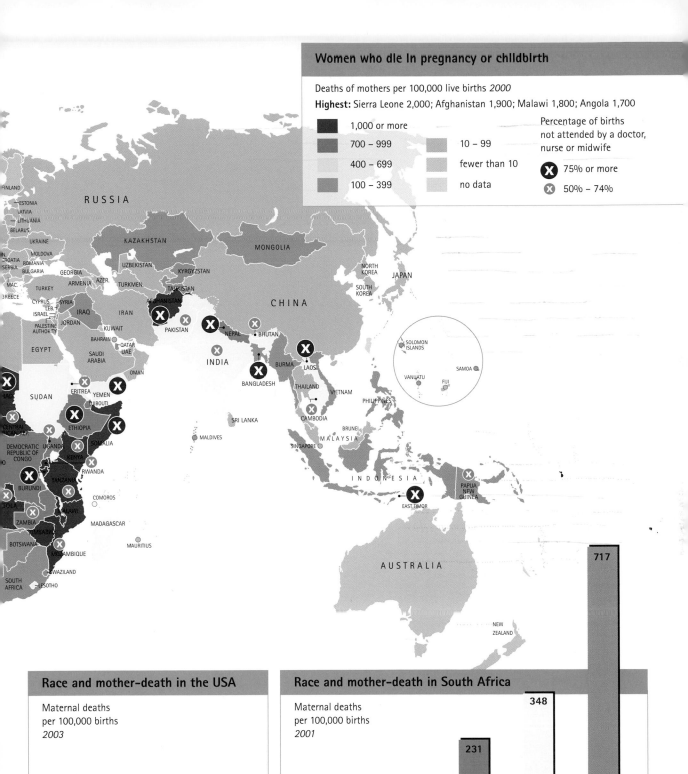

Women who die in pregnancy or childbirth

Deaths of mothers per 100,000 live births *2000*

Highest: Sierra Leone 2,000; Afghanistan 1,900; Malawi 1,800; Angola 1,700

- 1,000 or more
- 700 – 999
- 400 – 699
- 100 – 399
- 10 – 99
- fewer than 10
- no data

Percentage of births not attended by a doctor, nurse or midwife

- **X** 75% or more
- **X** 50% – 74%

Race and mother-death in the USA

Maternal deaths per 100,000 births *2003*

African/American	Hispanic	white
31	10	8

Race and mother-death in South Africa

Maternal deaths per 100,000 births *2001*

white/European	Indian/Asian	colored	black/African
79	231	348	717

41

13 Son Preference

Everywhere, boys tend to be privileged over girls. A cultural preference for sons over daughters is almost universal. But in a few places, this preference is acted out in ways that produce demographic distortion.

Sex ratios provide the surest evidence of extreme son preference. The biological norm is for about 95 girls to be born for every 100 boys, but boy infants have a naturally higher mortality rate so by early childhood the numbers should be roughly equal. In several countries, however, including South Korea, India, China, Bangladesh and Pakistan, the sex ratio is so severely skewed, with as few as 80 girls per 100 boys, that it is now causing widespread social distortions. Among other consequences, a shortage of women seems to be contributing to local and regional increases in trafficking and kidnapping of women (see also Map 19).

Son preference takes several forms, sometimes starting in the womb. In some places prenatal tests are used to detect female fetuses, which are then aborted. Such testing is prohibited in China, South Korea, and India, but these laws are weakly enforced. Female infanticide is common in some places, with girl infants killed within hours or days of birth. The neglect of girls – such as feeding them less or withholding medical attention – is chronic in many regions.

Son preference reflects the combined forces of economics, culture and religion. As smaller families become the norm, evidence suggests that the pressure to have sons accelerates. Girls are widely considered to have a lower economic value than boys – a view often strengthened by marriage, dowry, and inheritance practices. Son preference used to be thought of as a practice of the poor, but evidence suggests the opposite – increasing affluence magnifies perceptions of the greater worth of boys.

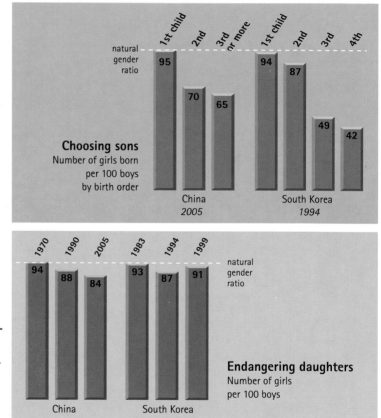

Choosing sons
Number of girls born per 100 boys by birth order

China 2005: 1st child 95, 2nd 70, 3rd or more 65
South Korea 1994: 1st child 94, 2nd 87, 3rd 49, 4th 42

natural gender ratio

Endangering daughters
Number of girls per 100 boys

China: 1970 – 94, 1990 – 88, 2005 – 84
South Korea: 1983 – 93, 1994 – 87, 1999 – 91

natural gender ratio

Missing girls

The discrepancy between the number of girls and women in the population and the number that would be expected if there were no discrimination.

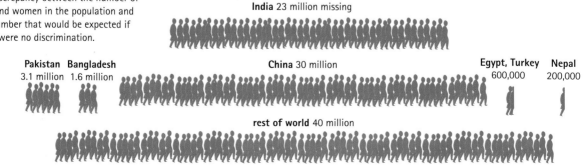

India 23 million missing

Pakistan 3.1 million   Bangladesh 1.6 million   China 30 million   Egypt, Turkey 600,000   Nepal 200,000

rest of world 40 million

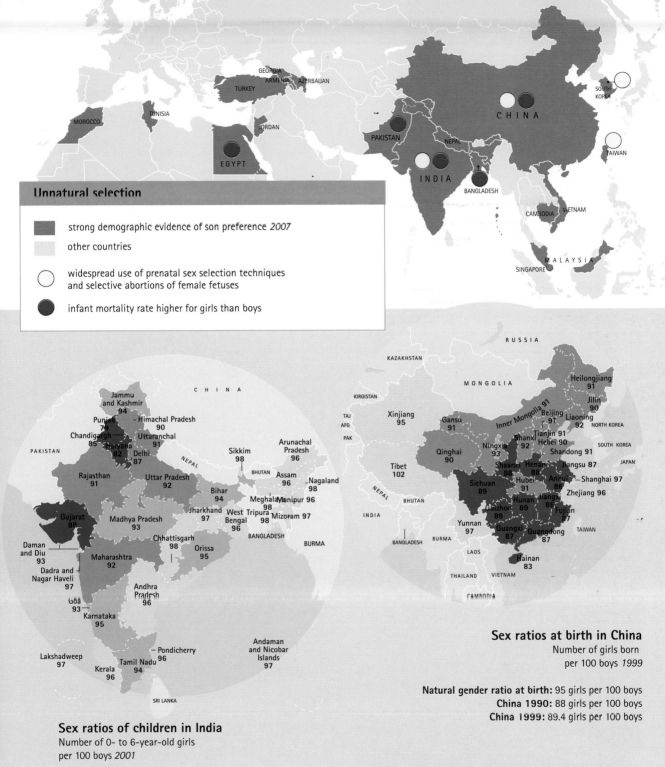

Unnatural selection

- strong demographic evidence of son preference *2007*
- other countries
- ○ widespread use of prenatal sex selection techniques and selective abortions of female fetuses
- ● infant mortality rate higher for girls than boys

Sex ratios of children in India
Number of 0- to 6-year-old girls
per 100 boys *2001*

**Natural gender ratio
of 0- to 6-year-olds:**
105 girls per 100 boys

India 1991: 94.5 girls per 100 boys
India 2001: 92.7 girls per 100 boys

India map values:
Jammu and Kashmir 94, Punjab 79, Himachal Pradesh 90, Chandigarh 85, Haryana 82, Uttaranchal 91, Delhi 87, Sikkim 98, Arunachal Pradesh 96, Rajasthan 91, Uttar Pradesh 92, Assam 96, Nagaland 98, Bihar 94, Meghalaya 98, Manipur 96, Gujarat 88, Madhya Pradesh 93, Jharkhand 97, West Bengal 96, Tripura 98, Mizoram 97, Daman and Diu 93, Chhattisgarh 98, Orissa 95, Dadra and Nagar Haveli 97, Maharashtra 92, Goa 93, Andhra Pradesh 96, Karnataka 95, Lakshadweep 97, Kerala 96, Tamil Nadu 94, Pondicherry 96, Andaman and Nicobar Islands 97

Sex ratios at birth in China
Number of girls born
per 100 boys *1999*

Natural gender ratio at birth: 95 girls per 100 boys
China 1990: 88 girls per 100 boys
China 1999: 89.4 girls per 100 boys

China map values:
Heilongjiang 91, Jilin 90, Liaoning 92, Inner Mongolia 91, Beijing 91, Xinjiang 95, Gansu 91, Ningxia 93, Shanxi 92, Tianjin 91, Hebei 90, Shandong 91, Qinghai 90, Shaanxi 88, Henan 88, Jiangsu 87, Shanghai 97, Tibet 102, Sichuan 89, Hubei 91, Anhui 86, Zhejiang 96, Guizhou 89, Hunan 89, Jiangxi 86, Fujian 87, Yunnan 97, Guangxi 87, Guangdong 87, Hainan 83

Evidence of son preference varies widely across India and China. The Punjab–Haryana–Himachal Pradesh belt in northwest India is sometimes dubbed "India's Bermuda Triangle" – where girls vanish without a trace. In 1991 two states and territories in India had ratios below 88 girls per 100 boys; in 2001 there were five. In China, son preference appears strongest in urban areas, where small-family policies are most vigorously enforced.

43

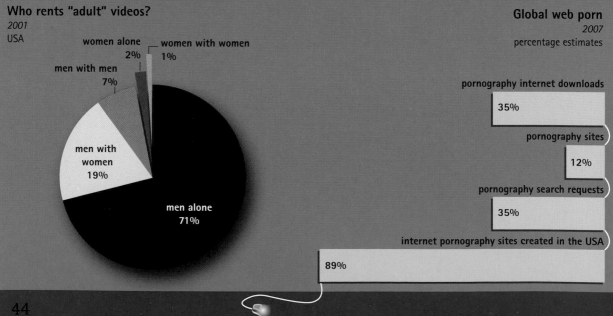

Who rents "adult" videos?
2001
USA

women alone
2%

women with women
1%

men with men
7%

men with women
19%

men alone
71%

Global web porn
2007
percentage estimates

pornography internet downloads
35%

pornography sites
12%

pornography search requests
35%

internet pornography sites created in the USA
89%

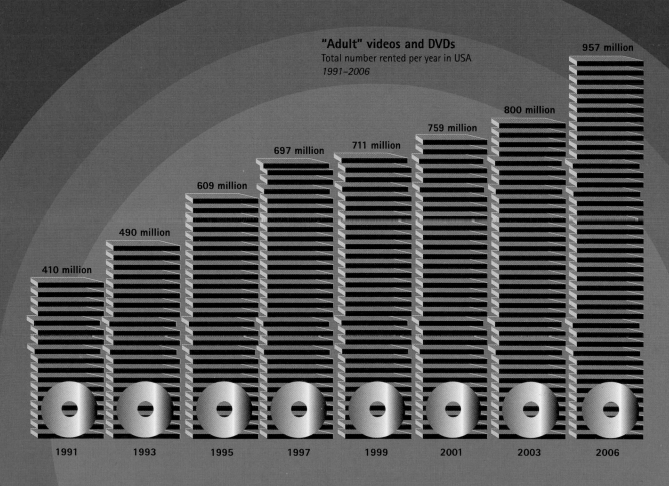

"Adult" videos and DVDs
Total number rented per year in USA
1991–2006

957 million

800 million

759 million

711 million

697 million

609 million

490 million

410 million

1991   1993   1995   1997   1999   2001   2003   2006

14 Breast Cancer

Breast cancer is the most common cancer among women. Worldwide over 1.5 million new cases are diagnosed each year. The incidence of breast cancer is highest in industrialized countries. Europe and North America, home to under one fifth of the world's women, account for half of the world's breast cancer cases. The lowest rates of breast cancer are found in Asia, but even in regions with low incidence the rates are increasing rapidly.

One in eight women in industrialized countries will develop breast cancer over an 85-year lifespan. Thirty years ago, this number was 1 in 20. Worldwide, breast cancer rates have increased 26 percent since 1980. Breast cancer activists are increasingly certain that environmental factors, including exposure to plastics-based estrogen-mimicking chemicals, are responsible for the near-epidemic rates of the disease.

In most of Western Europe and North America, the proportion of women who die from breast cancer has been steadily dropping since the late 1980s, a trend attributed to earlier diagnosis and better treatment. However, the benefits of advanced medical care are not evenly distributed. For example, in the USA, the diagnosed incidence of breast cancer is higher among white women than black, but black women are more likely to die from it. This difference is largely a function of unequal access to medical care.

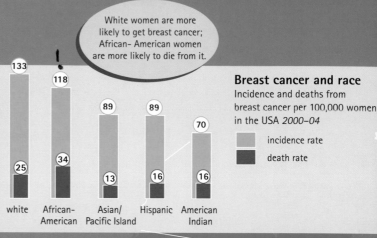

White women are more likely to get breast cancer; African- American women are more likely to die from it.

Breast cancer and race
Incidence and deaths from breast cancer per 100,000 women in the USA 2000–04

- incidence rate
- death rate

	white	African-American	Asian/Pacific Island	Hispanic	American Indian
incidence	133	118	89	89	70
death	25	34	13	16	16

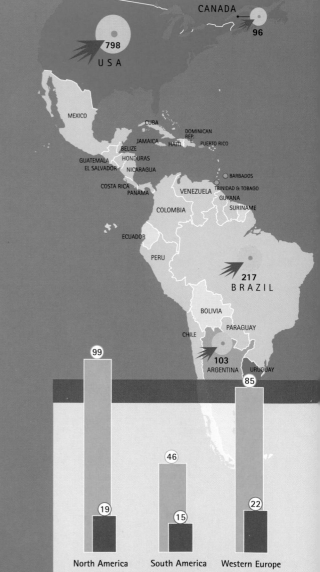

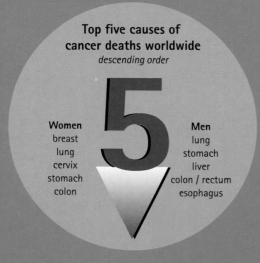

Top five causes of cancer deaths worldwide
descending order

5

Women	Men
breast	lung
lung	stomach
cervix	liver
stomach	colon / rectum
colon	esophagus

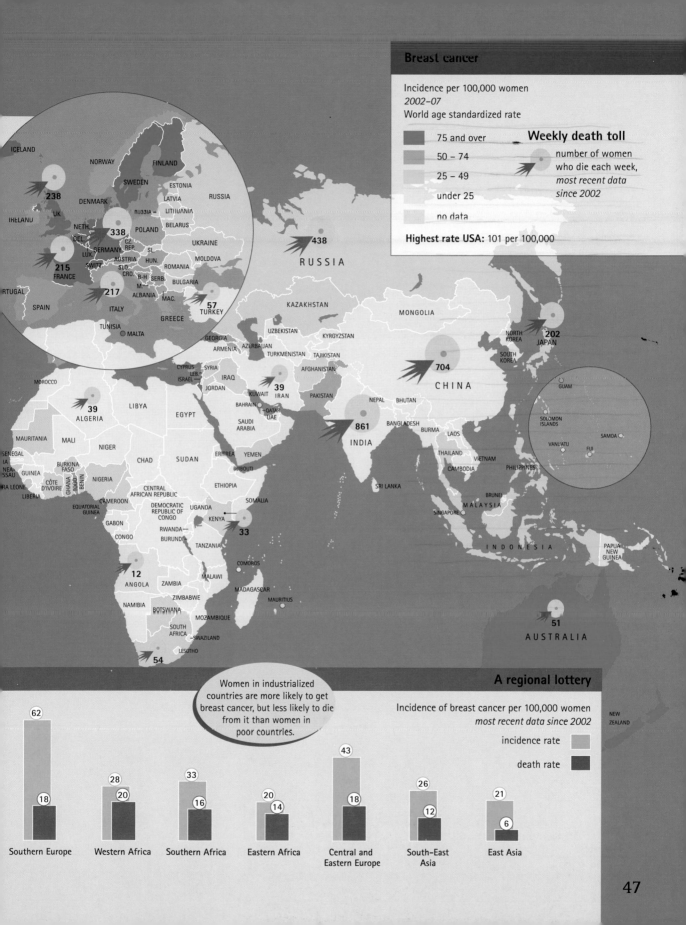

Breast cancer

Incidence per 100,000 women
2002–07
World age standardized rate

- 75 and over
- 50 – 74
- 25 – 49
- under 25
- no data

Weekly death toll

number of women who die each week, *most recent data since 2002*

Highest rate USA: 101 per 100,000

ICELAND
NORWAY
FINLAND
SWEDEN
ESTONIA
238 UK
DENMARK
LATVIA
RUSSIA
IRELAND
NETH.
BEL.
338 POLAND
BELARUS
LUX.
CZ. REP.
UKRAINE
GERMANY
SLO.
215 FRANCE
SWITZ.
AUSTRIA
HUN.
MOLDOVA
ROMANIA
SLO.
CRO.
B-H
SERB.
BULGARIA
217 ITALY
M.
ALBANIA
MAC.
57 TURKEY
PORTUGAL
SPAIN
GREECE
TUNISIA
MALTA

438
RUSSIA

KAZAKHSTAN
MONGOLIA

MOROCCO
GEORGIA
ARMENIA
AZERBAIJAN
UZBEKISTAN
KYRGYZSTAN
TURKMENISTAN
TAJIKISTAN

CYPRUS
LEB.
ISRAEL
SYRIA
IRAQ
JORDAN
AFGHANISTAN
39 IRAN
PAKISTAN

NORTH KOREA
SOUTH KOREA
202 JAPAN

LIBYA
EGYPT
KUWAIT
BAHRAIN
QATAR
UAE
SAUDI ARABIA
NEPAL
BHUTAN
704 CHINA

GUAM

SOLOMON ISLANDS

ALGERIA
39

861 INDIA
BANGLADESH
BURMA
LAOS
VANUATU
SAMOA
FIJI

MAURITANIA
MALI
NIGER
CHAD
SUDAN
ERITREA
YEMEN
DJIBOUTI
THAILAND
VIETNAM
CAMBODIA
PHILIPPINES

SENEGAL
GAMBIA
GUINEA BISSAU
GUINEA
SIERRA LEONE
LIBERIA
CÔTE D'IVOIRE
GHANA
TOGO
BENIN
NIGERIA
CAMEROON
CENTRAL AFRICAN REPUBLIC
ETHIOPIA
SRI LANKA
BRUNEI
MALAYSIA

SOMALIA
SINGAPORE
INDONESIA

EQUATORIAL GUINEA
GABON
CONGO
DEMOCRATIC REPUBLIC OF CONGO
UGANDA
RWANDA
BURUNDI
KENYA
33
TANZANIA

PAPUA NEW GUINEA

ANGOLA
12
ZAMBIA
MALAWI
COMOROS
MADAGASCAR
MAURITIUS

NAMIBIA
ZIMBABWE
BOTSWANA
MOZAMBIQUE

AUSTRALIA
51

SOUTH AFRICA
SWAZILAND
LESOTHO
54

NEW ZEALAND

A regional lottery

Women in industrialized countries are more likely to get breast cancer, but less likely to die from it than women in poor countries.

Incidence of breast cancer per 100,000 women
most recent data since 2002

- incidence rate
- death rate

Region	incidence	death
Southern Europe	62	18
Western Africa	28	20
Southern Africa	33	16
Eastern Africa	20	14
Central and Eastern Europe	43	18
South-East Asia	26	12
East Asia	21	6

Over 30 million adults in the world are HIV infected. Seventy percent of them live in Sub-Saharan Africa. More than half are women. Without access to the medical advances available in richer countries, most will die.

Women's social and sexual status puts them at particular risk of infection. Sexual relations between men and women are often framed by violence, coercion, and the presumption of men's "right" of sexual access to women. Many women are not able to negotiate safe sexual behavior with male partners. Higher illiteracy rates for women, and certain social arrangements such as polygamy add to their burden of risk.

Women, the traditional caretakers of families, often have no one to care for them when they are ill. The deaths of women leave whole households without support. Worldwide, a huge population of AIDS orphans, totaling an estimated 15 million children, has been left in the wake of the disease – 12 million of them in Sub-Saharan Africa. Girls who are orphaned are particularly vulnerable to sexual and economic exploitation and thus, in turn, to HIV infection.

Men are increasingly seeking young girls as sexual partners, presuming them to be safe from infection. This is both a local and global pattern: international trafficking in women (Map 19) increasingly involves ever-younger girls. Women are becoming infected on average at an age five to ten years younger than men.

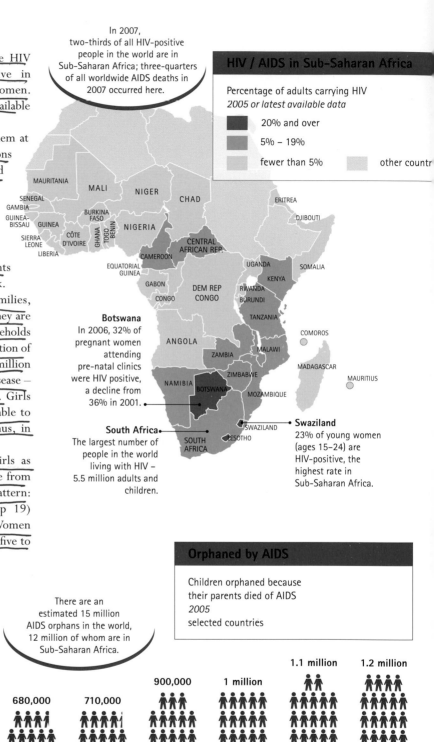

In 2007, two-thirds of all HIV-positive people in the world are in Sub-Saharan Africa; three-quarters of all worldwide AIDS deaths in 2007 occurred here.

HIV / AIDS in Sub-Saharan Africa

Percentage of adults carrying HIV
2005 or latest available data

- 20% and over
- 5% – 19%
- fewer than 5%
- other countr

Botswana
In 2006, 32% of pregnant women attending pre-natal clinics were HIV positive, a decline from 36% in 2001.

South Africa
The largest number of people in the world living with HIV – 5.5 million adults and children.

Swaziland
23% of young women (ages 15–24) are HIV-positive, the highest rate in Sub-Saharan Africa.

Orphaned by AIDS

Children orphaned because their parents died of AIDS
2005
selected countries

There are an estimated 15 million AIDS orphans in the world, 12 million of whom are in Sub-Saharan Africa.

120,000	450,000	550,000	680,000	710,000	900,000	1 million	1.1 million	1.2 million
Botswana, Burkina Faso, Burundi	Côte d'Ivoire	Malawi	Dem. Rep. Congo	Zambia	Nigeria	Uganda, Tanzania	Kenya, Zimbabwe	South Africa

In 2007, 31 million adults in the world were living with HIV; half of them are women.

Number of adults with HIV / AIDS
2006–07

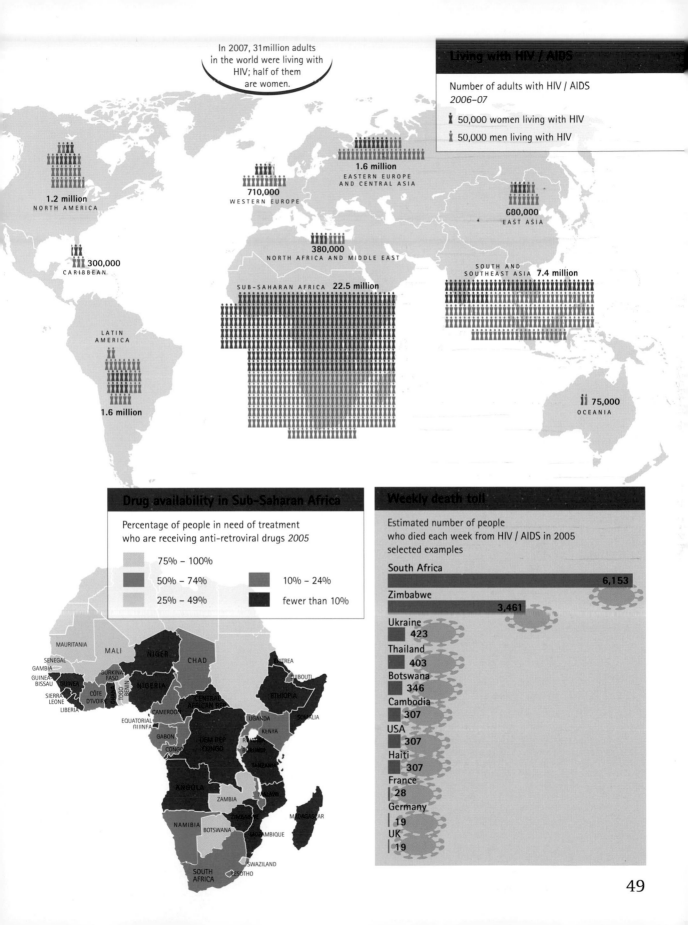

👤 50,000 women living with HIV

👤 50,000 men living with HIV

1.2 million
NORTH AMERICA

710,000
WESTERN EUROPE

1.6 million
EASTERN EUROPE
AND CENTRAL ASIA

600,000
EAST ASIA

300,000
CARIBBEAN

380,000
NORTH AFRICA AND MIDDLE EAST

SUB-SAHARAN AFRICA **22.5 million**

SOUTH AND
SOUTHEAST ASIA **7.4 million**

LATIN
AMERICA

1.6 million

75,000
OCEANIA

Drug availability in Sub-Saharan Africa

Percentage of people in need of treatment
who are receiving anti-retroviral drugs *2005*

- 75% – 100%
- 50% – 74%
- 25% – 49%
- 10% – 24%
- fewer than 10%

MAURITANIA
MALI
NIGER
CHAD
ERITREA
SENEGAL
GAMBIA
GUINEA-
BISSAU
GUINEA
BURKINA
FASO
NIGERIA
DJIBOUTI
SIERRA
LEONE
CÔTE
D'IVOIRE
TOGO
BENIN
CENTRAL
AFRICAN REP.
ETHIOPIA
LIBERIA
CAMEROON
SOMALIA
EQUATORIAL
GUINEA
UGANDA
KENYA
GABON
CONGO
DEM REP
CONGO
RWANDA
BURUNDI
TANZANIA
ANGOLA
MALAWI
ZAMBIA
MADAGASCAR
ZIMBABWE
NAMIBIA
BOTSWANA
MOZAMBIQUE
SWAZILAND
SOUTH
AFRICA
LESOTHO

Weekly death toll

Estimated number of people
who died each week from HIV / AIDS in 2005
selected examples

South Africa	6,153
Zimbabwe	3,461
Ukraine	423
Thailand	403
Botswana	346
Cambodia	307
USA	307
Haiti	307
France	28
Germany	19
UK	19

49

16 Sports

Notions of "appropriate" masculinity and femininity are deeply embedded within, and structured by, participation in sports and athletics. Men who do not show much interest in sports are often considered to be suspiciously unmanly; women who want to develop body strength and athletic skills still have an uphill struggle against conventional definitions of femininity. Athletic women and girls are often stigmatized and socially "policed" by being labeled as lesbians. In many countries, these conventional barriers and attitudes are changing – but only after decades of challenge by women sports pioneers, persistence by women who have long dealt with being "gender outcasts," and after prolonged legal battles.

The participation of women in the Olympics mirrors the larger struggle of women in sports. A gender gap remains in the money and media attention showered on men's and women's sports – even in sports where women have achieved prominence. It was only in 2007, for example, that the organizing committee for the Wimbledon Tennis Tournament agreed to pay equal prize money to female and male tennis competitors; the French Open equalized payments to women and men tennis singles champions in 2006; the US Open started offering equal prize money to women and men in 1968.

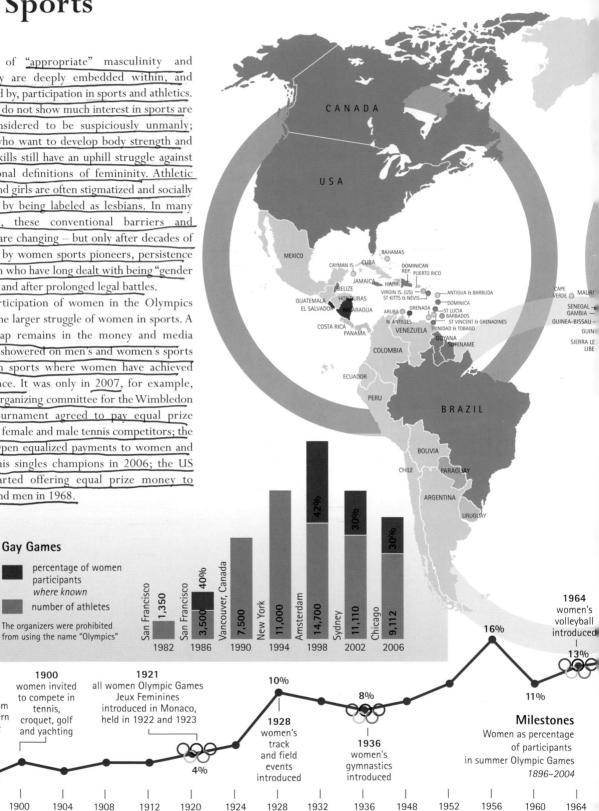

Gay Games

■ percentage of women participants *where known*

■ number of athletes

The organizers were prohibited from using the name "Olympics"

	San Francisco 1982	San Francisco 1986	Vancouver, Canada 1990	New York 1994	Amsterdam 1998	Sydney 2002	Chicago 2006
athletes	1,350	3,500	7,500	11,000	14,700	11,110	9,112
% women		40%			42%	30%	30%

Milestones
Women as percentage of participants in summer Olympic Games
1896–2004

1896 women barred from first modern Olympic Games — 0%

1900 women invited to compete in tennis, croquet, golf and yachting

1921 all women Olympic Games Jeux Feminines introduced in Monaco, held in 1922 and 1923 — 4%

1928 women's track and field events introduced — 10%

1936 women's gymnastics introduced — 8%

1964 women's volleyball introduced — 13%

16%   11%

1896 1900 1904 1908 1912 1920 1924 1928 1932 1936 1948 1952 1956 1960 1964

50 Copyright © Myriad Editions

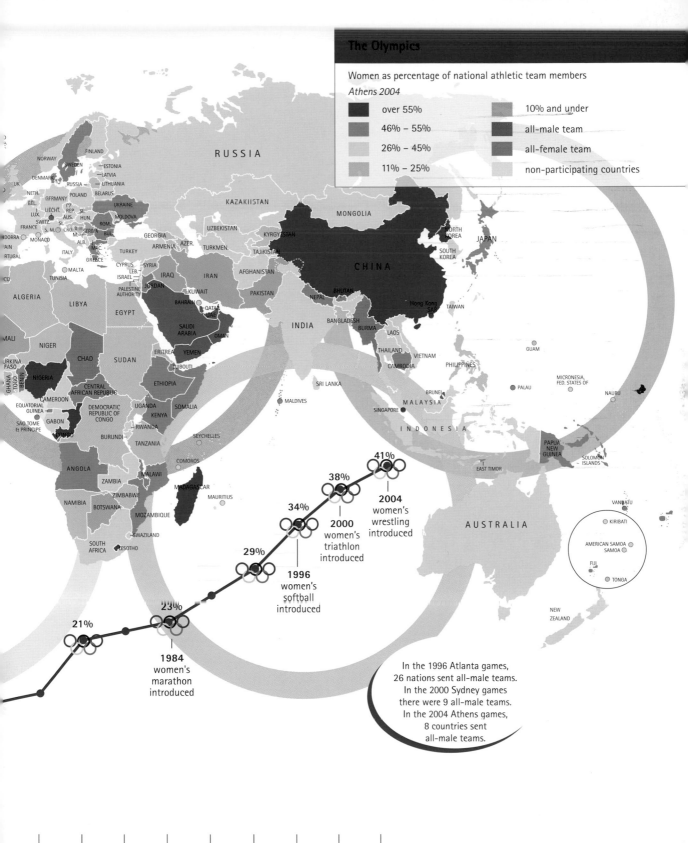

Women as percentage of national athletic team members
Athens 2004

- over 55%
- 46% – 55%
- 26% – 45%
- 11% – 25%
- 10% and under
- all-male team
- all-female team
- non-participating countries

NORWAY FINLAND
SWEDEN ESTONIA
DENMARK LATVIA
RUSSIA LITHUANIA
UK POLAND BELARUS
NETH. GERMANY
BEL. CZECH REP. UKRAINE KAZAKHSTAN
LUX. LIECHT. SL AUS. HUN. MOLDOVA
FRANCE SWITZ. SL ROM. UZBEKISTAN KYRGYZSTAN MONGOLIA
ANDORRA S.M. CRO. B.H. BUL. GEORGIA TURKMEN. TAJIKISTAN
MONACO ITALY SERBIA ARMENIA AZER.
PORTUGAL MAC. ALB. GREECE TURKEY AFGHANISTAN
SPAIN MALTA CYPRUS SYRIA IRAN CHINA
TUNISIA LEB. IRAQ JORDAN PAKISTAN NORTH KOREA
ALGERIA LIBYA ISRAEL PALESTINE KUWAIT NEPAL BHUTAN SOUTH KOREA JAPAN
AUTHORITY BAHRAIN QATAR UAE INDIA BANGLADESH TAIWAN
EGYPT SAUDI OMAN BURMA Hong Kong SAR
MALI NIGER ARABIA LAOS
BURKINA FASO CHAD SUDAN ERITREA YEMEN THAILAND VIETNAM PHILIPPINES GUAM
GHANA TOGO DJIBOUTI SRI LANKA CAMBODIA MICRONESIA,
BENIN NIGERIA CENTRAL ETHIOPIA MALDIVES FED. STATES OF
CAMEROON AFRICAN REPUBLIC BRUNEI NAURU
EQUATORIAL UGANDA SOMALIA MALAYSIA PALAU
GUINEA DEMOCRATIC KENYA SINGAPORE
SAO TOME REPUBLIC OF RWANDA I N D O N E S I A
& PRINCIPE GABON CONGO BURUNDI SEYCHELLES PAPUA SOLOMON
CONGO TANZANIA NEW ISLANDS
ANGOLA COMOROS GUINEA
MALAWI MADAGASCAR EAST TIMOR
ZAMBIA MAURITIUS VANUATU
NAMIBIA ZIMBABWE AUSTRALIA KIRIBATI
BOTSWANA MOZAMBIQUE AMERICAN SAMOA
SWAZILAND SAMOA
SOUTH LESOTHO FIJI
AFRICA NEW TONGA
ZEALAND

RUSSIA

41%
2004
women's
wrestling
introduced

38%

34%
2000
women's
triathlon
introduced

29%
1996
women's
softball
introduced

23%

21%

1984
women's
marathon
introduced

In the 1996 Atlanta games,
26 nations sent all-male teams.
In the 2000 Sydney games
there were 9 all-male teams.
In the 2004 Athens games,
8 countries sent
all-male teams.

| | 1972 | 1976 | 1980 | 1984 | 1988 | 1992 | 1996 | 2000 | 2004 |

International beauty contests promote and export a white, Western standard of beauty. Globalization is accelerating the adoption of these standards around the world. As new governments seek global economic integration, they often signal this by jumping on the Western beauty bandwagon. The proliferation of beauty contests in the former Soviet bloc countries is particularly striking.

There are now few places in the world untouched by the commerce of beauty. A handful of companies control the international cosmetics market.

Women undergo a staggering amount of suffering in the pursuit of beauty. Around the world, but especially in the rich countries, tens of thousands of women each year have their bodies cut, shaped, stapled, tucked, and manipulated to conform to prevailing standards of beauty. A preoccupation with weight and body image has become an intrinsic part of the lives of women and girls. This is particularly so in the USA, but eating disorders are also noticeably increasing in Europe, Japan, and the former Soviet Union.

Contestants first participating in Miss Universe or Miss World:

1991: Bulgaria, Romania, Russia, Ghana
1992: Croatia, Poland, Czechoslovakia, Hungary
1993: Estonia, Swaziland
1994: China, Slovakia, Zimbabwe
1995: Ukraine, Zambia, Seychelles
1997: Croatia
1998: Angola
1999: Botswana
2002: Vietnam
2005: Mongolia
2006: Cambodia

USA 2002
- 42% of girls in Grades 1–3 want to be thinner.
- 81% of 10-year-old girls are afraid of being fat.
- The average US model is thinner than 98% of all US women.
- 80% of 13-year-olds have attempted to lose weight.

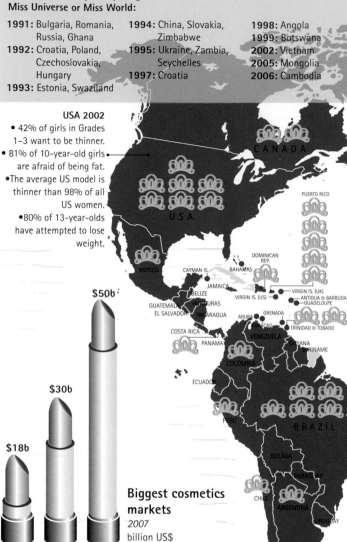

Biggest cosmetics markets
2007
billion US$

- Italy $10b
- China $12b
- UK $13b
- Germany $14b
- France $14b
- Brazil $18b
- Japan $30b
- USA $50b

Avon's world

2007

■ Avon products sold

Avon opened new markets in:
2000: Singapore, South Korea
2001: Greece Morocco
Since 2001: Albania, Armenia, Belarus, Bosnia & Herzegovina, Botswana, Bulgaria, Chile, Georgia, Guyana, Lesotho, Luxembourg, Macedonia, Montenegro, Mozambique, Namibia, Netherlands, Serbia, Swaziland, Switzerland, Turkmenistan, Uganda, Vietnam, Zambia

The beauty beat

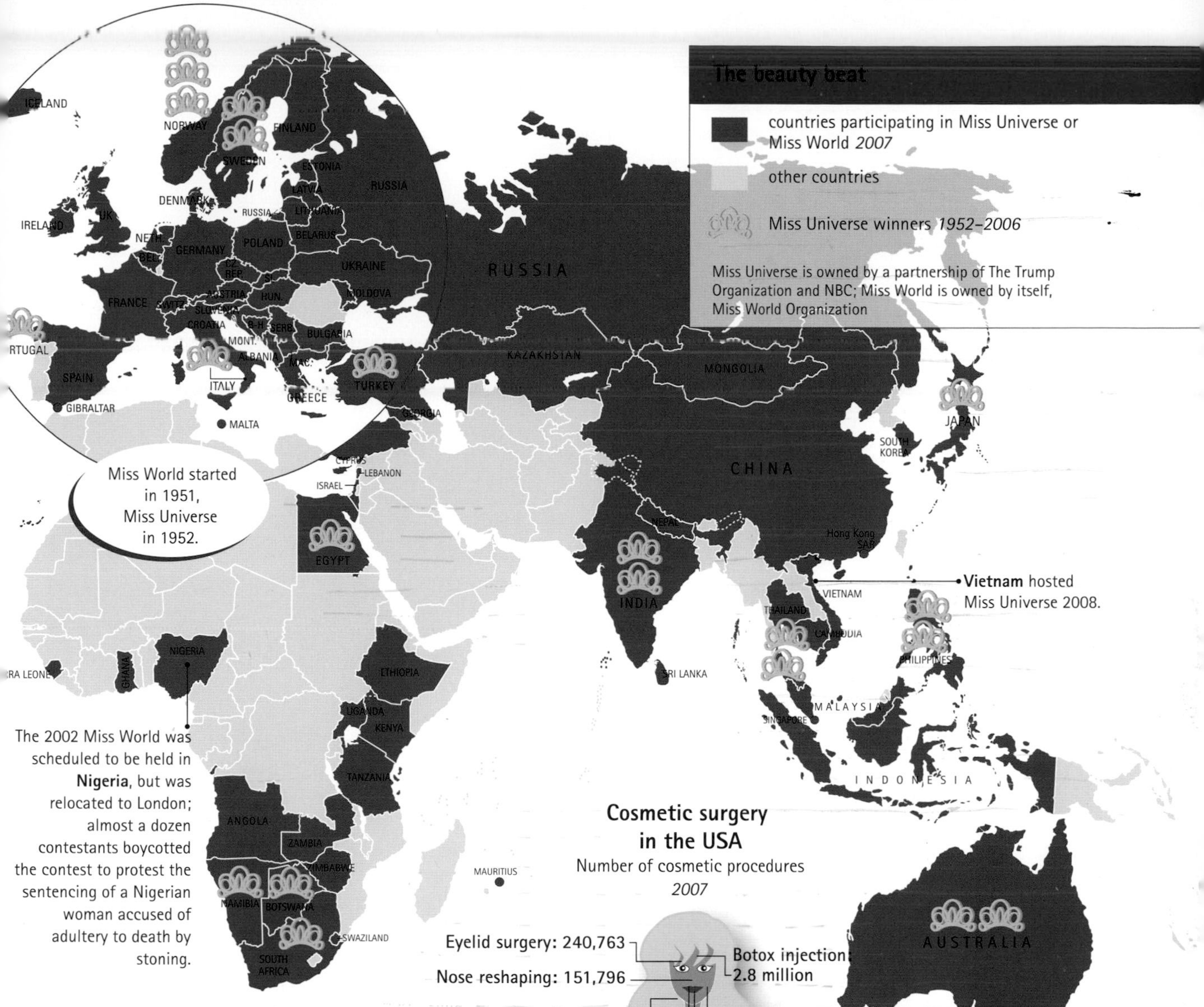

- ■ countries participating in Miss Universe or Miss World *2007*
- □ other countries
- Miss Universe winners *1952–2006*

Miss Universe is owned by a partnership of The Trump Organization and NBC; Miss World is owned by itself, Miss World Organization

Miss World started in 1951, Miss Universe in 1952.

The 2002 Miss World was scheduled to be held in **Nigeria**, but was relocated to London; almost a dozen contestants boycotted the contest to protest the sentencing of a Nigerian woman accused of adultery to death by stoning.

Vietnam hosted Miss Universe 2008.

Map labels: ICELAND, NORWAY, SWEDEN, FINLAND, ESTONIA, LATVIA, RUSSIA, DENMARK, IRELAND, UK, NETH., BEL., GERMANY, POLAND, LITHUANIA, BELARUS, UKRAINE, RUSSIA, FRANCE, SWITZ., AUSTRIA, HUN., SLOVAKIA, CROATIA, SLOVENIA, MOLDOVA, SERBIA, BULGARIA, MONT., ALBANIA, IRAQ, RTUGAL, SPAIN, GIBRALTAR, ITALY, GREECE, TURKEY, GEORGIA, MALTA, KAZAKHSTAN, MONGOLIA, CYPRUS, LEBANON, ISRAEL, EGYPT, NEPAL, CHINA, SOUTH KOREA, JAPAN, RA SIERRA LEONE, GHANA, NIGERIA, ETHIOPIA, UGANDA, KENYA, INDIA, VIETNAM, THAILAND, CAMBODIA, PHILIPPINES, SRI LANKA, HONG KONG SAR, ANGOLA, ZAMBIA, TANZANIA, ZIMBABWE, NAMIBIA, BOTSWANA, MALAYSIA, SINGAPORE, INDONESIA, SWAZILAND, SOUTH AFRICA, MAURITIUS, AUSTRALIA, NEW ZEALAND, RUSSIA

Cosmetic surgery in the USA
Number of cosmetic procedures *2007*

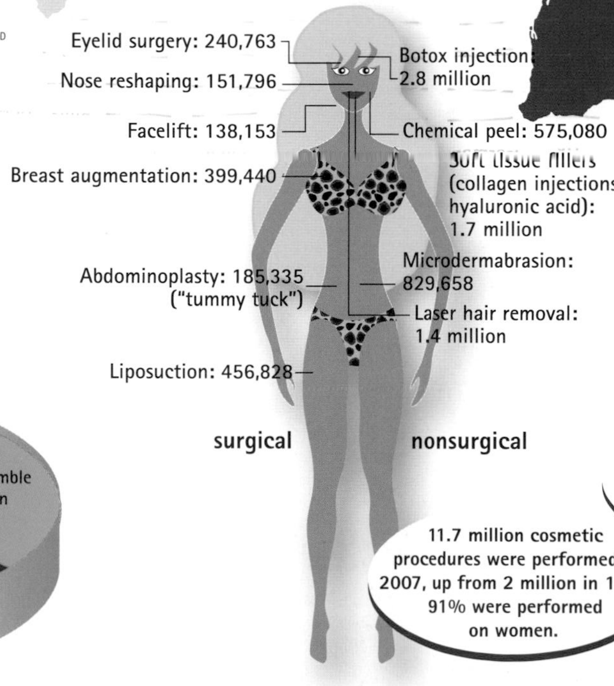

- Eyelid surgery: 240,763
- Nose reshaping: 151,796
- Facelift: 138,153
- Breast augmentation: 399,440
- Abdominoplasty: 185,335 ("tummy tuck")
- Liposuction: 456,828

- Botox injection: 2.8 million
- Chemical peel: 575,080
- Soft tissue fillers (collagen injections, hyaluronic acid): 1.7 million
- Microdermabrasion: 829,658
- Laser hair removal: 1.4 million

surgical   **nonsurgical**

Americans spent $13 billion on cosmetic procedures in 2006.

11.7 million cosmetic procedures were performed in 2007, up from 2 million in 1997. 91% were performed on women.

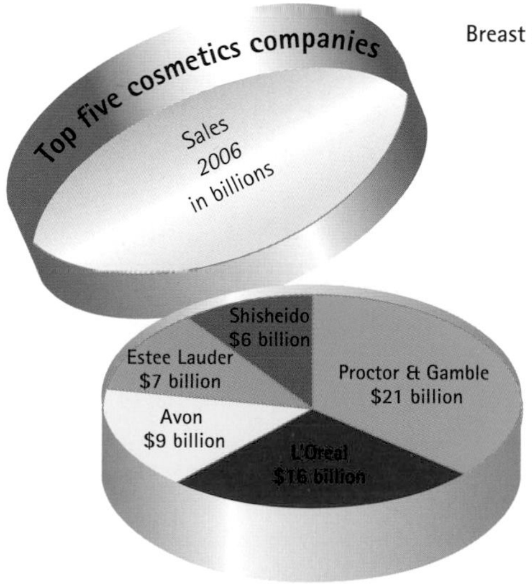

Top five cosmetics companies
Sales 2006 in billions

- Proctor & Gamble $21 billion
- L'Oreal $16 billion
- Avon $9 billion
- Estee Lauder $7 billion
- Shisheido $6 billion

18 | Under the Knife

Female genital mutilation (FGM), also called female circumcision or genital cutting, is extensively practiced in parts of Africa and the Middle East. Its practice and prevalence varies widely across these regions and within each country, although in some places FGM is nearly universal. FGM is found in cultures representing several religions, yet it is not required by any religious teaching. An estimated 130 million girls and women in the world have undergone genital cutting; each year, another 2 million join their ranks.

FGM is mostly performed on young girls. Its over-riding purpose is to ensure the desirability and suitability of women for marriage, in large part by controlling their sexual behavior. Female genital mutilation typically reduces women's sexual desire. Infibulation is a way of ensuring premarital virginity. In some cultures female genitalia are considered unclean, and the ritual of circumcision is thought to smooth and purify girls' bodies.

FGM has severe consequences for women's physical and mental health. However, the practice is so culturally embedded in some societies that it is proving difficult to challenge. Traditionally, it is women who perform the actual cutting, and many women are strong proponents of the practice. However, it is also women who have taken the lead in organizing against FGM. Most governments remain reluctant to intervene.

The prevalence of FGM has not changed much in the last decade, and some new worrying trends are evident. Possibly as a result of an emphasis on the negative health implications of FGM, there has been a dramatic increase in the proportion of FGM operations carried out by trained health-care personnel. This approach may reduce some of the immediate physical consequences of the procedure (such as pain and bleeding) but it also tends to obscure its human rights aspect and could hinder the development of long-term solutions for ending the practice. There has also been a lowering in some countries of the average age at which a girl is subjected to the procedure. This could be to some extent the result of anti-FGM legislation: the younger the girl, the easier it is to elude legal scrutiny.

One encouraging trend seen consistently is that women aged 15–19 years are less likely to have been submitted to FGM than are women in older age groups and support for ending the practice is particularly high among younger women.

CANADA

USA

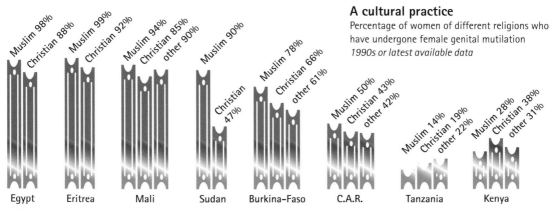

A cultural practice

Percentage of women of different religions who have undergone female genital mutilation
1990s or latest available data

Egypt — Muslim 98%, Christian 88%
Eritrea — Muslim 99%, Christian 92%
Mali — Muslim 94%, Christian 85%, other 90%
Sudan — Muslim 90%, Christian 47%
Burkina-Faso — Muslim 78%, Christian 66%, other 61%
C.A.R. — Muslim 50%, Christian 43%, other 42%
Tanzania — Muslim 14%, Christian 19%, other 22%
Kenya — Muslim 28%, Christian 38%, other 31%

Estimated prevalence of female genital mutilation
in girls and women 15–49 years
2001 or latest available data

almost universal: *90% or more*

common practice: *50% – 90%*

less common practice: *5% – 50%*

minor incidence: *less than 5%, often practiced only among
small groups or communities*

imported incidence: *practiced within some immigrant groups,
where known*

other countries

Egypt
90% of girls who have
undergone FGM were
under 14 years old at the
time. An estimated 90% of
FGM procedures are
performed by doctors or
other trained medical
personnel.

Mali
50% of girls who have
undergone FGM were under
5 years old when the
procedure was done.

The elimination
of FGM is called for in the
CEDAW treaty, the Convention on the
Rights of the Child, and by dozens of
international agencies including the
World Health Organization, UNICEF,
UNESCO, and UNIFEM.

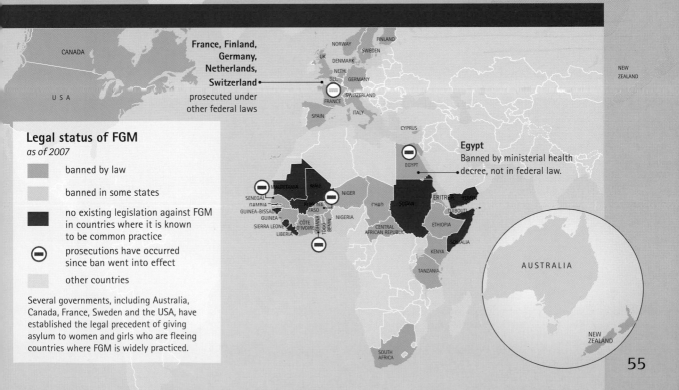

**France, Finland,
Germany,
Netherlands,
Switzerland**
prosecuted under
other federal laws

Egypt
Banned by ministerial health
decree, not in federal law.

Legal status of FGM
as of 2007

banned by law

banned in some states

no existing legislation against FGM
in countries where it is known
to be common practice

prosecutions have occurred
since ban went into effect

other countries

Several governments, including Australia,
Canada, France, Sweden and the USA, have
established the legal precedent of giving
asylum to women and girls who are fleeing
countries where FGM is widely practiced.

55

Women's bodies are commodities in the global sex trade, a multi-billion dollar industry.

The international sex trade thrives on economic disparity — between men and women at all scales, and between regions on a global scale. Globalization has heightened these disparities. New regions and countries enter into the sex trade as their economic fortunes wax or wane. As poverty deepens in Eastern Europe, it becomes a major source region for prostitutes; as wealth expands in China and Malaysia, men in those countries fuel an increased demand for the traffic in women and girls. Large circuits of trafficking operate among the countries of East and Southeast Asia, and from Central and Eastern Europe into Western Europe. The global sex trade is sustained by astounding levels of coercion, torture, rape, and systemic violence. Women are often lured into the sex trade under false pretences — hired as waitresses or maids and then forced into prostitution. Girls are often sold into prostitution by poor families and, increasingly, girls and women are simply kidnapped, often from poverty-stricken regions, to be traded globally as sex slaves and prostitutes.

The AIDS/HIV epidemic is fueling demand for younger and younger girls, as customers try to find "safe" commercial sex partners.

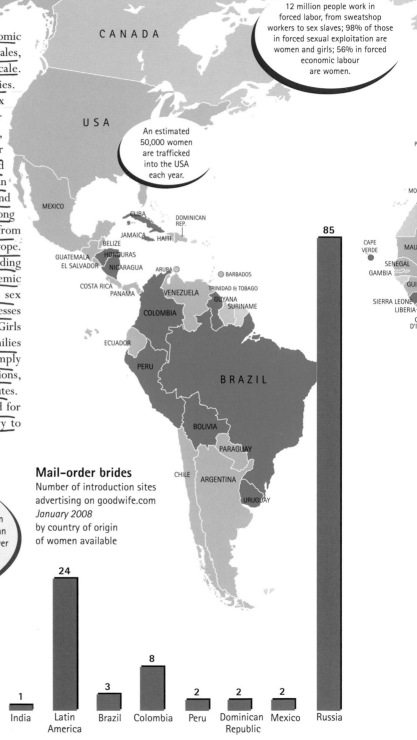

Worldwide 12 million people work in forced labor, from sweatshop workers to sex slaves; 98% of those in forced sexual exploitation are women and girls; 56% in forced economic labour are women.

An estimated 50,000 women are trafficked into the USA each year.

85

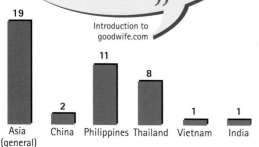

"We, as [Western] men, are more and more wanting to step back from the types of [Western] women we meet now. With many women taking on the 'me first' feminist agenda and the man continuing to take a back seat to her desire for power and control many men are turned off by this and look back to having a more traditional woman as our partner."

Introduction to goodwife.com

Mail-order brides
Number of introduction sites advertising on goodwife.com
January 2008
by country of origin
of women available

Asia (general)	China	Philippines	Thailand	Vietnam	India	Latin America	Brazil	Colombia	Peru	Dominican Republic	Mexico	Russia
19	2	11	8	1	1	24	3	8	2	2	2	85

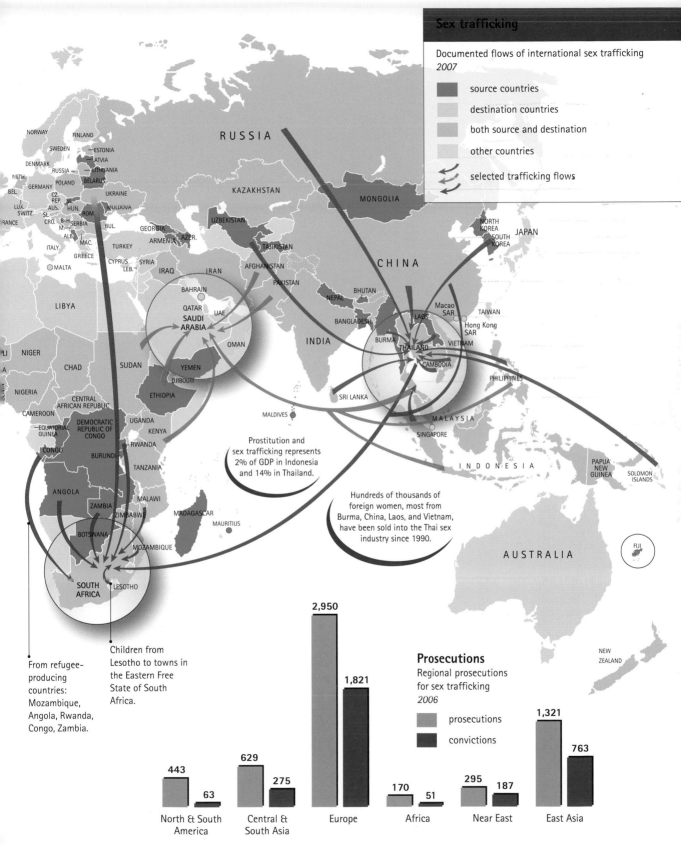

Documented flows of international sex trafficking
2007

- source countries
- destination countries
- both source and destination
- other countries
- selected trafficking flows

Prostitution and sex trafficking represents 2% of GDP in Indonesia and 14% in Thailand.

Hundreds of thousands of foreign women, most from Burma, China, Laos, and Vietnam, have been sold into the Thai sex industry since 1990.

From refugee-producing countries: Mozambique, Angola, Rwanda, Congo, Zambia.

Children from Lesotho to towns in the Eastern Free State of South Africa.

Prosecutions

Regional prosecutions for sex trafficking
2006

- prosecutions
- convictions

Region	prosecutions	convictions
North & South America	443	63
Central & South Asia	629	275
Europe	2,950	1,821
Africa	170	51
Near East	295	187
East Asia	1,321	763

20 Rape

Women everywhere live under the threat of rape – often a threat greatest in their own homes and from men they know. In many countries, feminists are successfully changing the legal status of rape and the judicial treatment of victims to reflect the understanding that rape is not "having sex"; rape is violence intended to assert male power and control. Nonetheless, rape remains a grievously under-reported crime – because social stigma is typically attached to the victim as much as, or more than, it is to the perpetrator. Estimates suggest that the actual incidence of rape may be up to 50 times the numbers reported. In most countries, rape within marriage is not a crime.

Rape is often exercised as a "privilege" of power. Institutional rape is a widespread problem – of prisoners by jail guards and police, of patients by hospital attendants, of refugees by authorities in refugee camps. Rape in war (see Map 38) is at epidemic proportions.

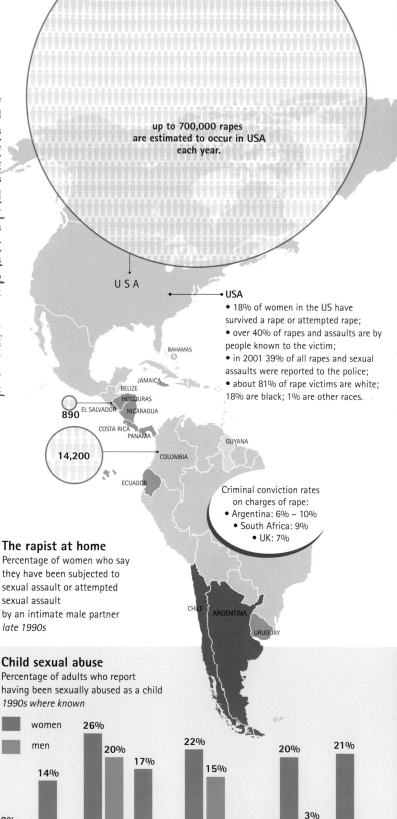

up to 700,000 rapes
are estimated to occur in USA
each year.

USA

USA
- 18% of women in the US have survived a rape or attempted rape;
- over 40% of rapes and assaults are by people known to the victim;
- in 2001 39% of all rapes and sexual assaults were reported to the police;
- about 81% of rape victims are white; 18% are black; 1% are other races.

BAHAMAS

JAMAICA
BELIZE
HONDURAS
EL SALVADOR NICARAGUA
890
COSTA RICA
PANAMA
GUYANA

14,200

COLOMBIA

ECUADOR

Criminal conviction rates
on charges of rape:
- Argentina: 6% – 10%
- South Africa: 9%
- UK: 7%

CHILE   ARGENTINA

URUGUAY

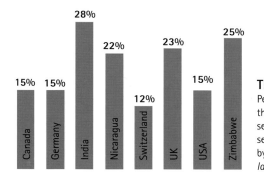

15%	15%	28%	22%	12%	23%	15%	25%
Canada	Germany	India	Nicaragua	Switzerland	UK	USA	Zimbabwe

The rapist at home
Percentage of women who say they have been subjected to sexual assault or attempted sexual assault
by an intimate male partner
late 1990s

Child sexual abuse
Percentage of adults who report having been sexually abused as a child
1990s where known

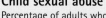
  women
  men

Antigua	Australia	Barbados	Canada	Costa Rica	Malaysia	New Zealand	Nicaragua	Norway	Spain	Switzerland	USA
11%	20%	30%	13% / 4%	32% / 13%	8% / 2%	14%	26% / 20%	17% / 1%	22% / 15%	20% / 3%	21%

Copyright © Myriad Editions

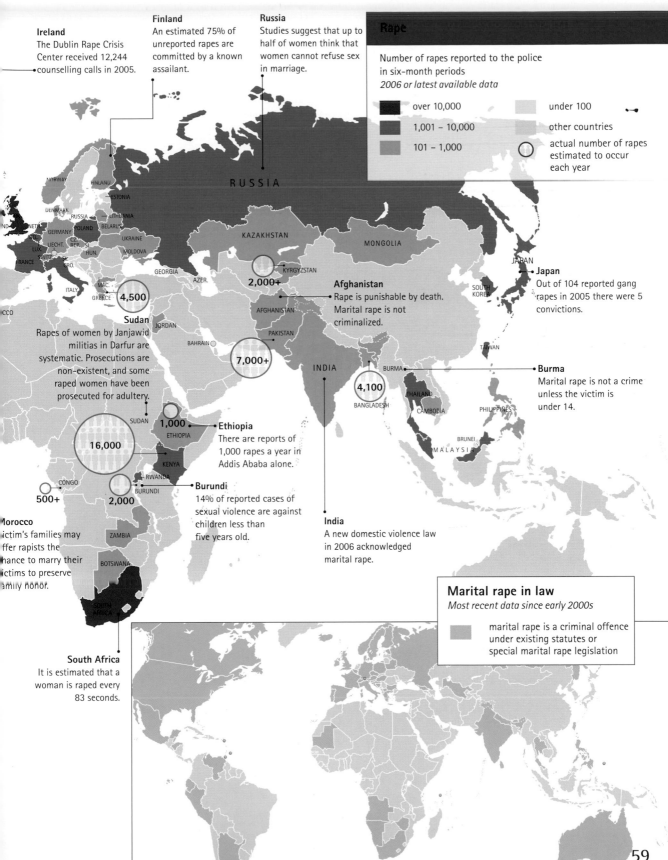

Ireland
The Dublin Rape Crisis Center received 12,244 counselling calls in 2005.

Finland
An estimated 75% of unreported rapes are committed by a known assailant.

Russia
Studies suggest that up to half of women think that women cannot refuse sex in marriage.

Rape

Number of rapes reported to the police in six-month periods
2006 or latest available data

over 10,000	under 100
1,001 – 10,000	other countries
101 – 1,000	actual number of rapes estimated to occur each year

NORWAY
FINLAND
DENMARK
RUSSIA
ESTONIA
LITHUANIA
GERMANY POLAND BELARUS
CZ. REP. SL.
LIECHT. HUN. UKRAINE
SWITZ. CRO. MOLDOVA
FRANCE
LUX.
BEL.
NETH.

RUSSIA

KAZAKHSTAN

MONGOLIA

JAPAN

Japan
Out of 104 reported gang rapes in 2005 there were 5 convictions.

SOUTH KOREA

GEORGIA
AZER.
2,000+ KYRGYZSTAN

Afghanistan
Rape is punishable by death. Marital rape is not criminalized.

ITALY
MAC.
GREECE **4,500**
Sudan
Rapes of women by Janjawid militias in Darfur are systematic. Prosecutions are non-existent, and some raped women have been prosecuted for adultery.

JORDAN
BAHRAIN ○
AFGHANISTAN
PAKISTAN
7,000+

INDIA

BURMA
TAIWAN

Burma
Marital rape is not a crime unless the victim is under 14.

BANGLADESH
4,100
THAILAND
CAMBODIA
PHILIPPINES

SUDAN
1,000
ETHIOPIA
Ethiopia
There are reports of 1,000 rapes a year in Addis Ababa alone.

16,000
KENYA

BRUNEI
MALAYSIA

CONGO
500+
RWANDA
BURUNDI
2,000
Burundi
14% of reported cases of sexual violence are against children less than five years old.

India
A new domestic violence law in 2006 acknowledged marital rape.

Morocco
ictim's families may ffer rapists the hance to marry their ictims to preserve amily honor.

ZAMBIA

BOTSWANA

SOUTH AFRICA

South Africa
It is estimated that a woman is raped every 83 seconds.

Marital rape in law
Most recent data since early 2000s

	marital rape is a criminal offence under existing statutes or special marital rape legislation

Household decision–makers
Percentage of women who say their husband alone makes decisions on household spending
2000–04
selected countries

Sub-Saharan Africa

Country	Percentage
Malawi	66%
Nigeria	65%
Mali	64%
Burkina Faso	56%
Uganda	53%
Tanzania	46%
Rwanda	43%
Cameroon	39%
Kenya	38%
Mozambique	36%
Benin	33%
Ghana	32%
Eritrea	27%
Zimbabwe	16%
Madagascar	6%

East Asia/Pacific

Philippines	9%
Indonesia	2%

CEE/CIS

Armenia	18%
Turkmenistan	11%

Latin America and Caribbean

Colombia	14%
Peru	11%
Haiti	10%
Bolivia	7%

South Asia

Bangladesh	34%
Nepal	30%

Middle East and North Africa

Morocco	34%
Jordan	31%
Egypt	24%

Worldwide, more and more women are working outside the home for pay, but they do so under quite different circumstances than men. They are typically paid less than men for their labor. This earnings discrepancy reflects several factors: outright gender discrimination, the concentration of women in female-dominated jobs, and the higher percentage of women working part-time.

The wage gap persists across sectors. In the high-prestige, high-pay internet sector in the USA, for example, women earn 24 percent less on average than their male counterparts. Everywhere, gender differences are magnified by racial and ethnic discrimination.

wage gap

Equal-pay legislation can prove effective in narrowing the earnings gap if it is seriously implemented. Even then the gender gap in wages persists because such legislation primarily dictates equal pay for the same job, but men and women typically work in different jobs ("occupational segregation").

Many women's waged work is in the informal sector – domestic service, or market trading, for example. This type of work is especially important in poorer countries and is usually a larger source of employment for women than for men.

Data on workforce participation must be treated with caution. The picture of women's work that can be drawn from official statistics is, at best, partial. What is officially counted as "work" is itself highly contested.

> In the USA
> 47% of daughters, compared with 35% of sons, born to parents on the bottom income rungs remain there as adults.

USA 2006
As a proportion of white men's earnings, white women earn 74%, African-American women earn 64% and Hispanic-American women earn 52%.

CANADA 73%

USA

95% BERMUDA

84% MEXICO

BAHAMAS
CUBA

DOMINICAN REP. 91%

JAMAICA HAITI

81% GUATEMALA BELIZE HONDURAS

91% GUADELOUPE
MARTINIQUE
ST LUCIA

EL SALVADOR NICARAGUA

ST VINCENT & GRENADINES BARBADOS

TRINIDAD & TOBAGO

98% COSTA RICA

VENEZUELA

GUYANA
SURINAME

PANAMA 96%

78% COLOMBIA

ECUADOR

PERU

82% BRAZIL

BOLIVIA

69% PARAGUAY

CHILE ARGENTINA

URUGUAY

Lost childhoods
Percentage of children aged 5–14 engaged in child labor
2006

boys
girls

CARIBBEAN — 12% / 10%

WEST & CENTRAL AFRICA — 33% / 34%

CENTRAL EASTERN EUROPE/CIS — 5% / 5%

MIDDLE EAST & NORTH AFRICA — 10% / 8%

SUB-SAHARAN AFRICA — 36% / 34%

EASTERN & SOUTHERN AFRICA — 38% / 33%

SOUTH ASIA — 14% / 12%

EAST ASIA & PACIFIC — 11% / 10%

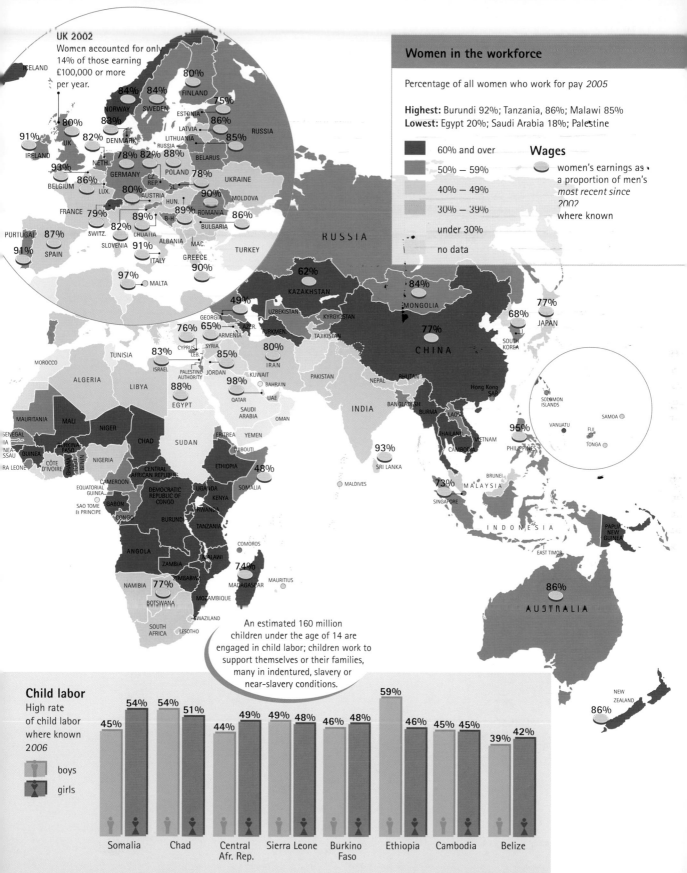

UK 2002
Women accounted for only 14% of those earning £100,000 or more per year.

Women in the workforce

Percentage of all women who work for pay *2005*

Highest: Burundi 92%; Tanzania, 86%; Malawi 85%
Lowest: Egypt 20%; Saudi Arabia 18%; Palestine

60% and over	
50% – 59%	
40% – 49%	
30% – 39%	
under 30%	
no data	

Wages
women's earnings as a proportion of men's *most recent since 2002* where known

ICELAND

91% IRELAND
80% UK
84% NORWAY 84% SWEDEN 80% FINLAND
83% DENMARK 75% ESTONIA
82% 86% LATVIA 85% RUSSIA
78% NETH. 82% RUSSIA 88% LITHUANIA
93% 80% GERMANY CZ REP. 82% POLAND 78% BELARUS
86% BELGIUM LUX. HUN. UKRAINE
79% FRANCE 89% 90% MOLDOVA
82% AUSTRIA SL 89% ROMANIA 86%
89% SWITZ. B-H BULGARIA
87% PORTUGAL 91% SLOVENIA CROATIA ALBANIA MAC.
91% SPAIN 91% ITALY 90% GREECE
97% MALTA TURKEY

62% KAZAKHSTAN
84% MONGOLIA
77% JAPAN
68% SOUTH KOREA
77% CHINA
49% UZBEKISTAN KYRGYZSTAN
76% GEORGIA 65% ARMENIA AZER. TAJIKISTAN
TURKMEN.
83% CYPRUS LEB. 85% SYRIA 80% IRAN
ISRAEL JORDAN PALESTINE AUTHORITY
88% EGYPT 98% KUWAIT BAHRAIN QATAR UAE
SAUDI ARABIA OMAN PAKISTAN
NEPAL BHUTAN INDIA BANGLADESH BURMA

MOROCCO
ALGERIA LIBYA
TUNISIA
MAURITANIA MALI NIGER CHAD SUDAN ERITREA YEMEN
SENEGAL GUINEA-BISSAU NEA GUINEA BURKINA FASO NIGERIA DJIBOUTI
SIERRA LEONE CÔTE D'IVOIRE GHANA TOGO BENIN CENTRAL AFRICAN REPUBLIC ETHIOPIA 48% SOMALIA
EQUATORIAL GUINEA CAMEROON UGANDA KENYA
SAO TOME & PRINCIPE GABON CONGO DEMOCRATIC REPUBLIC OF CONGO RWANDA
BURUNDI TANZANIA
ANGOLA ZAMBIA MALAWI COMOROS
NAMIBIA ZIMBABWE 74% MADAGASCAR MAURITIUS
77% BOTSWANA MOZAMBIQUE
SWAZILAND
SOUTH AFRICA LESOTHO

93% SRI LANKA
MALDIVES

THAILAND VIETNAM CAMBODIA LAOS
95% PHILIPPINES
BRUNEI
73% SINGAPORE MALAYSIA
INDONESIA
EAST TIMOR PAPUA NEW GUINEA

Hong Kong SAR

SOLOMON ISLANDS
VANUATU SAMOA
FIJI
TONGA

86% AUSTRALIA

NEW ZEALAND 86%

An estimated 160 million children under the age of 14 are engaged in child labor; children work to support themselves or their families, many in indentured, slavery or near-slavery conditions.

Child labor
High rate of child labor where known *2006*

- boys
- girls

	Somalia	Chad	Central Afr. Rep.	Sierra Leone	Burkino Faso	Ethiopia	Cambodia	Belize
boys	45%	54%	44%	49%	46%	59%	45%	39%
girls	54%	51%	49%	48%	48%	46%	45%	42%

Women are both "segregated" and "concentrated" in the workforce. They are employed in different occupations from men, and are over-represented in a limited number of occupations. Despite the entry of more women into the waged workforce, they are still entering the workforce in a small range of jobs. Everywhere in the world, there are "women's jobs" and "men's jobs", although the definition of these change over time and from place to place.

Generally, more women than men work in the services sector, and fewer women than men work in the industrial sector. The notable exception to this is the "global assembly line." The recent expansion of globalized industrial production –

the shift of low-wage industrial production from core economies to developing countries – relies almost entirely on women's labor. Global manufacturing companies take advantage of the fact that women in poor countries have the most limited employment opportunities – and thus are the cheapest labor force available.

In the oldest Export Processing Zones (EPZs) the nature of industrial production is shifting, and the proportion of women workers is dropping: in the 1990s, about 80 percent of the employees in EPZs in Mexico and Malaysia were women; by 2000 the proportion in both countries had dropped to about 60 percent.

Industrial work

More than 20%
of economically active women
are employed
in the industrial sector
2003

Highest: Sri Lanka 35%;
Macedonia 30%;
Bulgaria 29%

Service work

More than 75%
of economically active women
are employed
in the service sector
2003

Highest: Saudi Arabia 98%;
Qatar, Suriname 97%;
Bahamas 94%

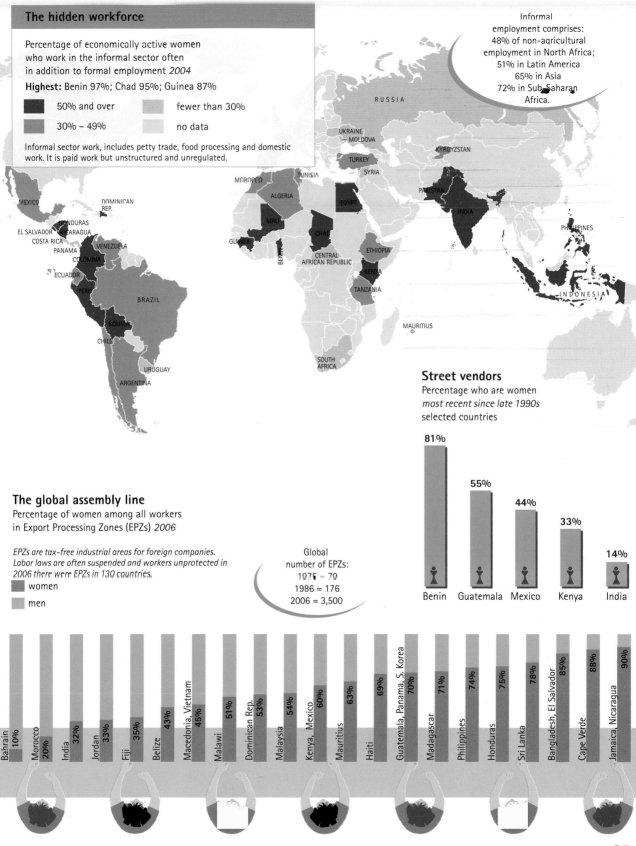

The hidden workforce

Percentage of economically active women
who work in the informal sector often
in addition to formal employment *2004*

Highest: Benin 97%; Chad 95%; Guinea 87%

- 50% and over
- 30% – 49%
- fewer than 30%
- no data

Informal sector work, includes petty trade, food processing and domestic
work. It is paid work but unstructured and unregulated.

Informal
employment comprises:
48% of non-agricultural
employment in North Africa;
51% in Latin America
65% in Asia
72% in Sub-Saharan
Africa.

Street vendors

Percentage who are women
most recent since late 1990s
selected countries

- Benin 81%
- Guatemala 55%
- Mexico 44%
- Kenya 33%
- India 14%

The global assembly line

Percentage of women among all workers
in Export Processing Zones (EPZs) *2006*

*EPZs are tax-free industrial areas for foreign companies.
Labor laws are often suspended and workers unprotected in
2006 there were EPZs in 130 countries.*

- women
- men

Global
number of EPZs:
1975 = 79
1986 = 176
2006 = 3,500

- Bahrain 10%
- Morocco 20%
- India 32%
- Jordan 33%
- Fiji 35%
- Belize 43%
- Macedonia, Vietnam 45%
- Malawi 51%
- Dominican Rep. 53%
- Malaysia 54%
- Kenya, Mexico 60%
- Mauritius 63%
- Haiti 69%
- Guatemala, Panama, S. Korea 70%
- Madagascar 71%
- Philippines 74%
- Honduras 75%
- Sri Lanka 78%
- Bangladesh, El Salvador 85%
- Cape Verde 88%
- Jamaica, Nicaragua 90%

65

The nature of women's participation in the waged labor force is shaped by many factors, including marriage, reproductive rights, and the widely prevailing expectation that women have primary responsibility for family care. Women everywhere have to balance "family" and "work" demands in ways that men seldom do. In most countries, they get little help doing so. One of the ways women manage is to work part-time; the feminization of part-time work is accelerating.

Feminists often describe women in the workforce as being "caught between the sticky floor and the glass ceiling" – concentrated in low-pay, low-status sectors on the one hand, and prevented from breaking into the top ranks on the other. Despite some modest gains in the past decade, the glass ceiling remains firmly in place. Women remain dramatically under-represented in the highest- paid, highest-prestige sectors of the workforce. Their fastest route to the top is often to start their own companies: in the USA, women-owned firms are growing at double the rate of firms owned by men.

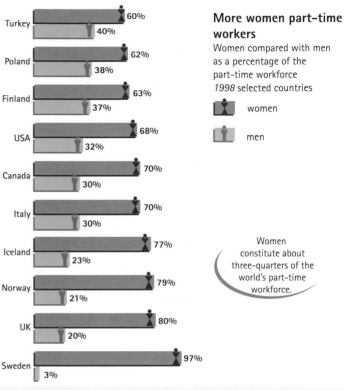

More women part-time workers

Women compared with men as a percentage of the part-time workforce
1998 selected countries

women

men

Women constitute about three-quarters of the world's part-time workforce.

Turkey 60% / 40%
Poland 62% / 38%
Finland 63% / 37%
USA 68% / 32%
Canada 70% / 30%
Italy 70% / 30%
Iceland 77% / 23%
Norway 79% / 21%
UK 80% / 20%
Sweden 97% / 3%

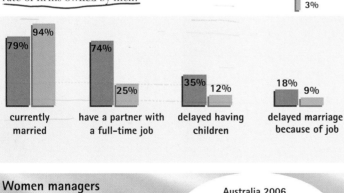

Combining work and family

Data based on a global survey of executives from North America, Latin America and Asia/Pacific
2003

women
men

- currently married: 79% / 94%
- have a partner with a full-time job: 74% / 25%
- delayed having children: 35% / 12%
- delayed marriage because of job: 18% / 9%
- decided not to have children: 12% / 1%

Women managers

Women as percentage of managers in the labor force
2007
selected developed economies

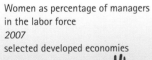

Australia 2006
Among ASX2000 companies, women held 12% of positions as executive managers. They represented 7% of top earners among these companies.

Norway 2008
A 2003 law required all public companies to have at least 40% women board directors by 2008. In 2003 7% of board directors were female; by January 2008 36% were female.

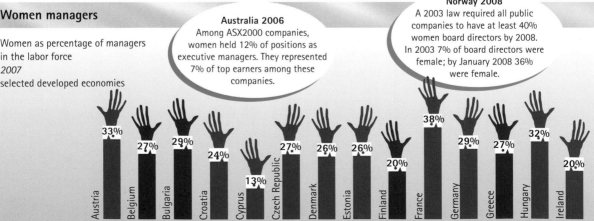

- Austria 33%
- Belgium 27%
- Bulgaria 29%
- Croatia 24%
- Cyprus 13%
- Czech Republic 27%
- Denmark 26%
- Estonia 26%
- Finland 20%
- France 38%
- Germany 29%
- Greece 27%
- Hungary 32%
- Ireland 20%

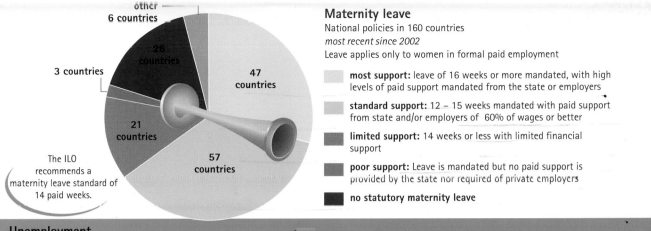

Maternity leave
National policies in 160 countries
most recent since 2002
Leave applies only to women in formal paid employment

other
6 countries

26 countries

3 countries

47 countries

21 countries

57 countries

The ILO recommends a maternity leave standard of 14 paid weeks.

most support: leave of 16 weeks or more mandated, with high levels of paid support mandated from the state or employers

standard support: 12 – 15 weeks mandated with paid support from state and/or employers of 60% of wages or better

limited support: 14 weeks or less with limited financial support

poor support: Leave is mandated but no paid support is provided by the state nor required of private employers

no statutory maternity leave

Unemployment

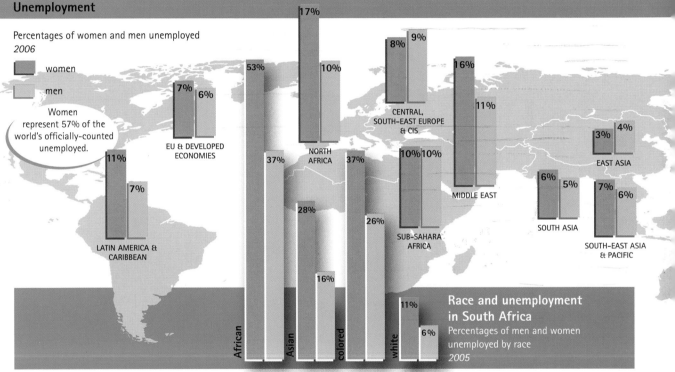

Percentages of women and men unemployed
2006

- women
- men

Women represent 57% of the world's officially-counted unemployed.

EU & DEVELOPED ECONOMIES 7% 6%

LATIN AMERICA & CARIBBEAN 11% 7%

NORTH AFRICA 17% 10%

CENTRAL, SOUTH-EAST EUROPE & CIS 8% 9%

MIDDLE EAST 16% 11%

SUB-SAHARA AFRICA 10% 10%

EAST ASIA 3% 4%

SOUTH ASIA 6% 5%

SOUTH-EAST ASIA & PACIFIC 7% 6%

Race and unemployment in South Africa
Percentages of men and women unemployed by race
2005

- African 53% 37%
- Asian 28% 16%
- colored 37% 26%
- white 11% 6%

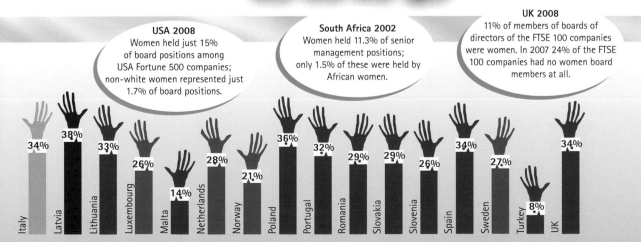

USA 2008
Women held just 15% of board positions among USA Fortune 500 companies; non-white women represented just 1.7% of board positions.

South Africa 2002
Women held 11.3% of senior management positions; only 1.5% of these were held by African women.

UK 2008
11% of members of boards of directors of the FTSE 100 companies were women. In 2007 24% of the FTSE 100 companies had no women board members at all.

Italy	Latvia	Lithuania	Luxembourg	Malta	Netherlands	Norway	Poland	Portugal	Romania	Slovakia	Slovenia	Spain	Sweden	Turkey	UK
34%	38%	33%	26%	14%	28%	21%	36%	32%	29%	29%	26%	34%	27%	8%	34%

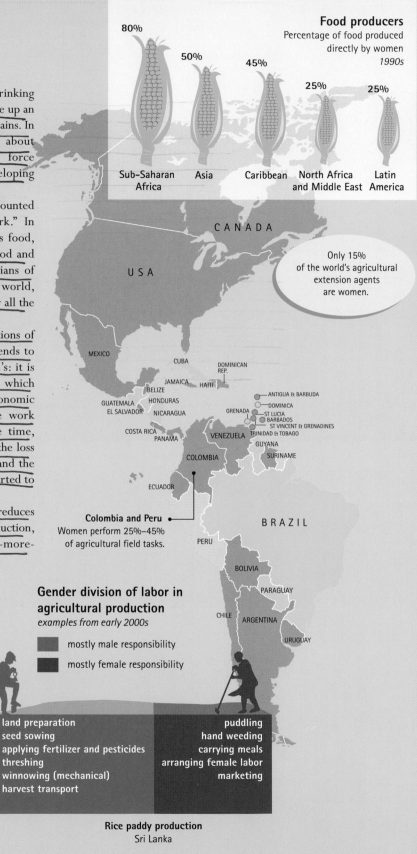

The world's agricultural labor force is shrinking year by year. But as it shrinks, women make up an increasing share of the labor force that remains. In official statistics, women make up about 40 percent of the agricultural labor force worldwide – about 67 percent in developing countries.

But much of women's farm work is uncounted hidden under the rubric of "housework." In addition to growing much of the world's food, women's specialized knowledge about food and agriculture makes them essential custodians of biodiversity. In most of the developing world, women grow, harvest and prepare virtually all the food consumed by their families.

Modernization alters the gendered relations of agricultural production. Mechanization tends to reduce men's farm labor, but not women's: it is mostly deployed to produce cash crops, which men usually control; it opens up new economic opportunities for men, and shifts male work patterns away from home. At the same time, women's farm work increases because of the loss of men's help in subsistence production and the loss of control over crops that may have started to be profitable.

Commercialization of agriculture often reduces the land available for subsistence crop production, and leaves women to cultivate ever-more-marginal lands.

Food producers
Percentage of food produced directly by women
1990s

Sub-Saharan Africa	Asia	Caribbean	North Africa and Middle East	Latin America
80%	50%	45%	25%	25%

Only 15% of the world's agricultural extension agents are women.

Colombia and Peru
Women perform 25%–45% of agricultural field tasks.

Gender division of labor in agricultural production
examples from early 2000s

- ■ mostly male responsibility
- ■ mostly female responsibility

Wheat production
South Erishilipu village, Northwest China

mostly male responsibility	mostly female responsibility
ploughing	weeding
planting	fertilizing
spraying	processing
	storage

Rice paddy production
Sri Lanka

mostly male responsibility	mostly female responsibility
land preparation	puddling
seed sowing	hand weeding
applying fertilizer and pesticides	carrying meals
threshing	arranging female labor
winnowing (mechanical)	marketing
harvest transport	

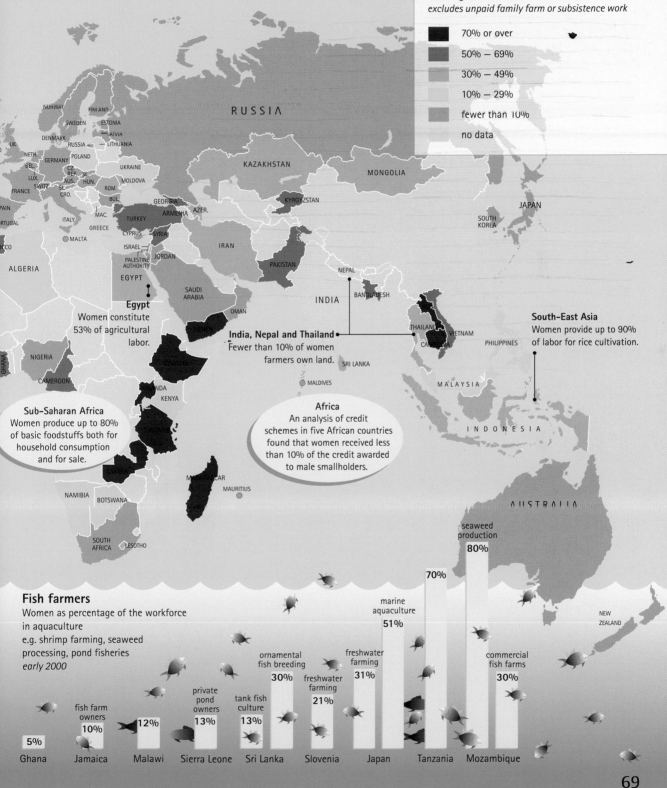

Agricultural work

Percentage of economically active women working in the agricultural sector *1995–2005*
excludes unpaid family farm or subsistence work

- 70% or over
- 50% – 69%
- 30% – 49%
- 10% – 29%
- fewer than 10%
- no data

Egypt
Women constitute 53% of agricultural labor.

India, Nepal and Thailand
Fewer than 10% of women farmers own land.

South-East Asia
Women provide up to 90% of labor for rice cultivation.

Sub-Saharan Africa
Women produce up to 80% of basic foodstuffs both for household consumption and for sale.

Africa
An analysis of credit schemes in five African countries found that women received less than 10% of the credit awarded to male smallholders.

Fish farmers

Women as percentage of the workforce in aquaculture
e.g. shrimp farming, seaweed processing, pond fisheries
early 2000

								seaweed production **80%**	
							marine aquaculture		
						freshwater farming	**70%**		
				ornamental fish breeding		**31%**	**51%**		commercial fish farms
				30%	freshwater farming				**30%**
			private pond owners	tank fish culture	**21%**				
	fish farm owners	**12%**	**13%**	**13%**					
5%	**10%**								
Ghana	Jamaica	Malawi	Sierra Leone	Sri Lanka	Slovenia	Japan	Tanzania	Mozambique	

69

Both men and women work for more hours than conventional measurements suggest. The unpaid labor of sustaining families and households, for example, represents a substantial part of daily work that is usually overlooked in official accounts. Feminists have long pressed for an overhaul in the ways "work" is measured. One alternative way to assess the different activities of men and women is to study time use. A "time-budgets" approach to measuring men's and women's contributions to household and national productivity reveals work that is done in the informal and unpaid sector, work that is rendered invisible in official work statistics.

Time-budget studies show that women spend much more of their time than men in informal, unpaid, and household production work. Most of men's total worktime is paid, most of women's is not. Overall, women work more hours each day than men, rest less, and perform a greater variety of tasks. The pattern starts early in life: in most countries, girl children do more work, especially in the home, than boys.

Women and girls everywhere have greater responsibility for household work: it is women who tend the goats, till the family garden, collect water, shop for food, prepare meals, wash clothes, look after aging parents, and keep the home clean. A large share of women's unpaid work is household labor. Women and men who share a household often do not share household labor. Attempts to change this allocation of household labor are at the center of personal and political struggles over gender roles, and are often fiercely resisted.

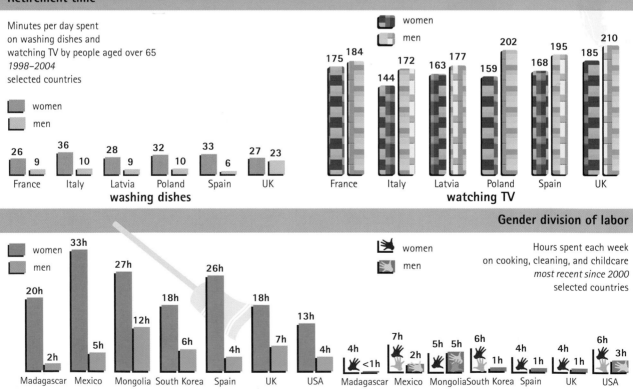

Retirement time

Minutes per day spent
on washing dishes and
watching TV by people aged over 65
1998–2004
selected countries

women
men

washing dishes

	France	Italy	Latvia	Poland	Spain	UK
women	26	36	28	32	33	27
men	9	10	9	10	6	23

watching TV

	France	Italy	Latvia	Poland	Spain	UK
women	175	144	163	159	168	185
men	184	172	177	202	195	210

Gender division of labor

Hours spent each week
on cooking, cleaning, and childcare
most recent since 2000
selected countries

women
men

housework

	Madagascar	Mexico	Mongolia	South Korea	Spain	UK	USA
women	20h	33h	27h	18h	26h	18h	13h
men	2h	5h	12h	6h	4h	7h	4h

childcare

	Madagascar	Mexico	Mongolia	South Korea	Spain	UK	USA
women	4h	7h	5h	6h	4h	4h	6h
men	<1h	2h	5h	1h	1h	1h	3h

Map values:
CANADA 60%
USA 58%
MEXICO 77%
NICARAGUA
URUGUAY 67%

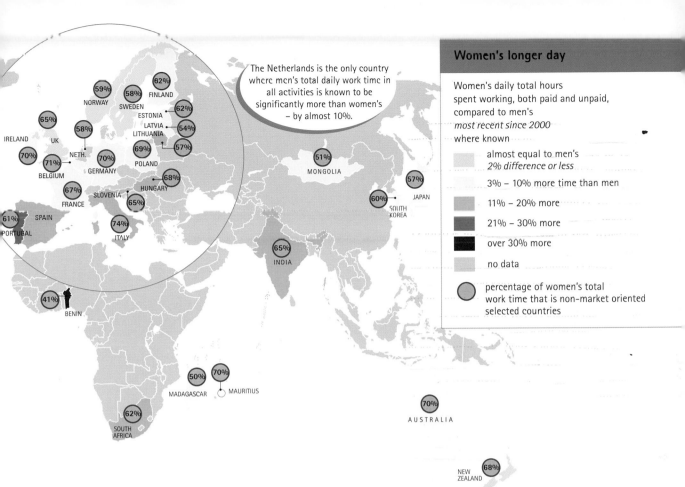

The Netherlands is the only country where men's total daily work time in all activities is known to be significantly more than women's – by almost 10%.

Women's longer day

Women's daily total hours spent working, both paid and unpaid, compared to men's
most recent since 2000
where known

- almost equal to men's *2% difference or less*
- 3% – 10% more time than men
- 11% – 20% more
- 21% – 30% more
- over 30% more
- no data

percentage of women's total work time that is non-market oriented selected countries

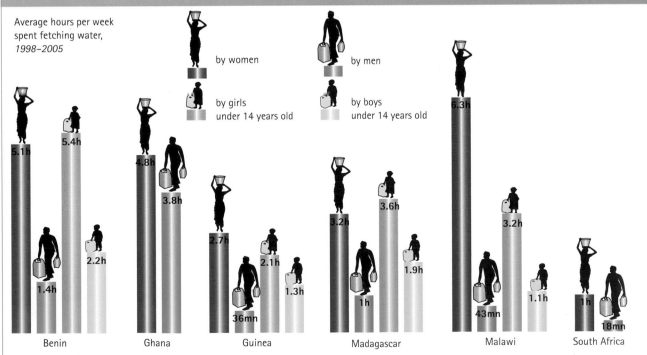

Water carriers

Average hours per week spent fetching water, *1998–2005*

by women
by men
by girls under 14 years old
by boys under 14 years old

Benin — 5.1h, 1.4h, 5.4h, 2.2h
Ghana — 4.8h, 3.8h
Guinea — 2.7h, 36mn, 2.1h, 1.3h
Madagascar — 3.2h, 1h, 3.6h, 1.9h
Malawi — 6.3h, 43mn, 3.2h, 1.1h
South Africa — 1h, 18mn

71

26 Migration

Economic globalization is accelerating the flow of migrant labor. About 200 million workers and their dependents work in countries outside their own. Asia is the largest source region of labor migrants. Every year several million Asians go overseas for jobs. Women outnumber men as migrants from the Philippines and Sri Lanka, and are a growing share of migrants from elsewhere.

Women working overseas tend to be concentrated in a few occupations, especially domestic help, labor-intensive factory production, and "entertainment". The "maid trade" is a distinct form of labor migration from poorer to richer countries. In the mid-2000s, more than 2 million women were working outside their own countries as foreign maids. The demand from rich countries for nurses is sapping health care in many poor countries.

Some labor-exporting governments encourage out-migration, while others try to stem the tide, partly in response to publicity about the abuse of women domestics overseas. Sex traffickers (see Map 19) often lure women into their circuits by tapping into legitimate migration streams.

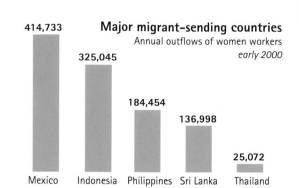

Major migrant-sending countries
Annual outflows of women workers
early 2000

414,733	325,045	184,454	136,998	25,072
Mexico	Indonesia	Philippines	Sri Lanka	Thailand

Labor to the Middle East
Between 30,000 and 50,000 nurses and teachers a year leave India, South Korea, Sri Lanka and Philippines to work in the Middle East.

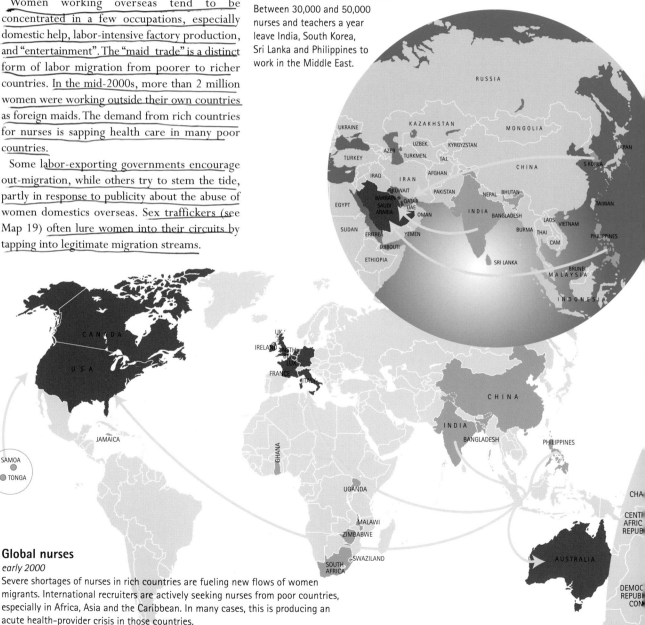

Global nurses
early 2000
Severe shortages of nurses in rich countries are fueling new flows of women migrants. International recruiters are actively seeking nurses from poor countries, especially in Africa, Asia and the Caribbean. In many cases, this is producing an acute health-provider crisis in those countries.

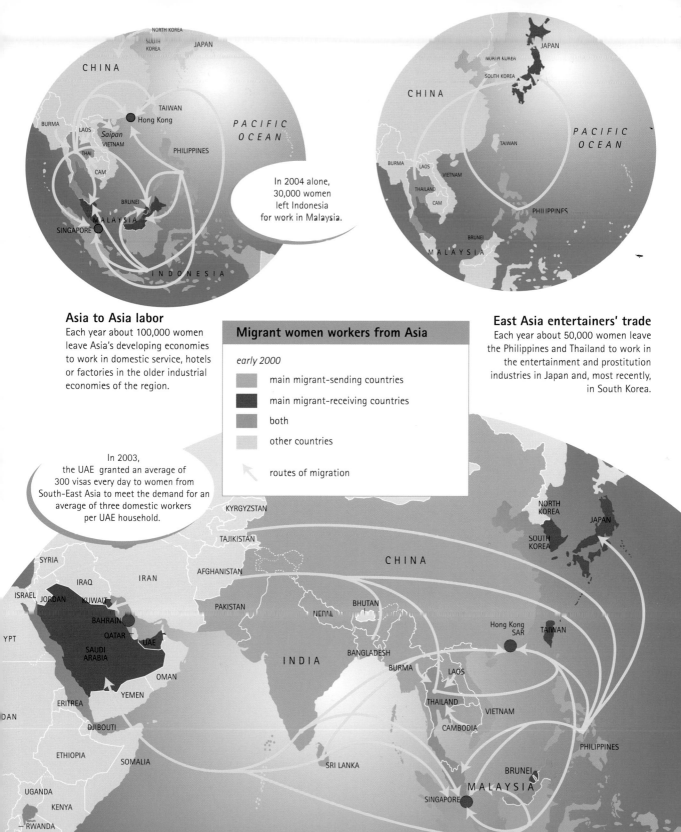

In 2004 alone, 30,000 women left Indonesia for work in Malaysia.

Asia to Asia labor

Each year about 100,000 women leave Asia's developing economies to work in domestic service, hotels or factories in the older industrial economies of the region.

East Asia entertainers' trade

Each year about 50,000 women leave the Philippines and Thailand to work in the entertainment and prostitution industries in Japan and, most recently, in South Korea.

Migrant women workers from Asia

early 2000

- main migrant-sending countries
- main migrant-receiving countries
- both
- other countries

→ routes of migration

In 2003, the UAE granted an average of 300 visas every day to women from South-East Asia to meet the demand for an average of three domestic workers per UAE household.

73

Part Six

TO HAVE AND HAVE NOT

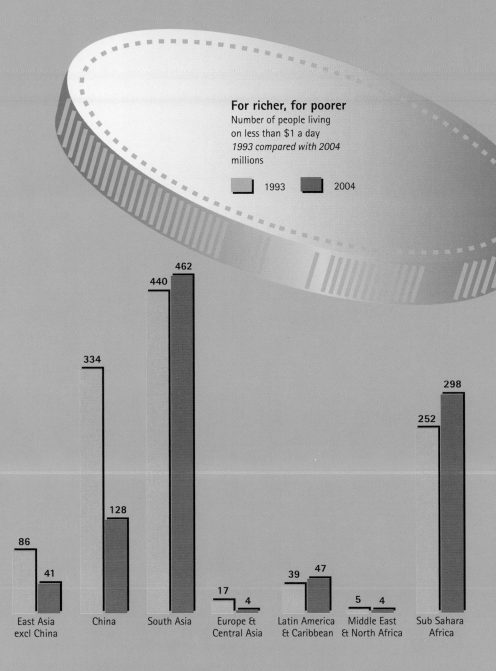

For richer, for poorer
Number of people living
on less than $1 a day
1993 compared with 2004
millions

1993   2004

East Asia excl China	86 / 41	
China	334 / 128	
South Asia	440 / 462	
Europe & Central Asia	17 / 4	
Latin America & Caribbean	39 / 47	
Middle East & North Africa	5 / 4	
Sub Sahara Africa	252 / 298	

27 Water

The lack of safe water and sanitation is the world's single largest cause of illness. Globally, over one billion people do not have access to improved water supply sources and more than two billion people do not have access to any type of improved sanitation facility.

The absence of adequate sanitation affects women and girls differently than men and boys. After puberty, girls are much less likely to attend schools that do not have adequate sanitation facilities; many schools in poor countries have no toilets at all. Child-bearing and family caretaking are all more dangerous without access to adequate sanitation. Lack of safe water makes women's household work even more arduous and complicated. In many countries women and girls are most vulnerable to attack when they have to use open, insecure, shared or distant sanitation facilities, especially at night.

Women and girls are the "water haulers" of the world (see Map 25). On average, women and girls in developing countries walk six kilometers a day, carrying 20 liters of water, greatly reducing the time they have for other activities. For girls, the burden of collecting water is a major factor in explaining their lower rates of participation in education: school attendance rates for girls are very sensitive to distance to water sources.

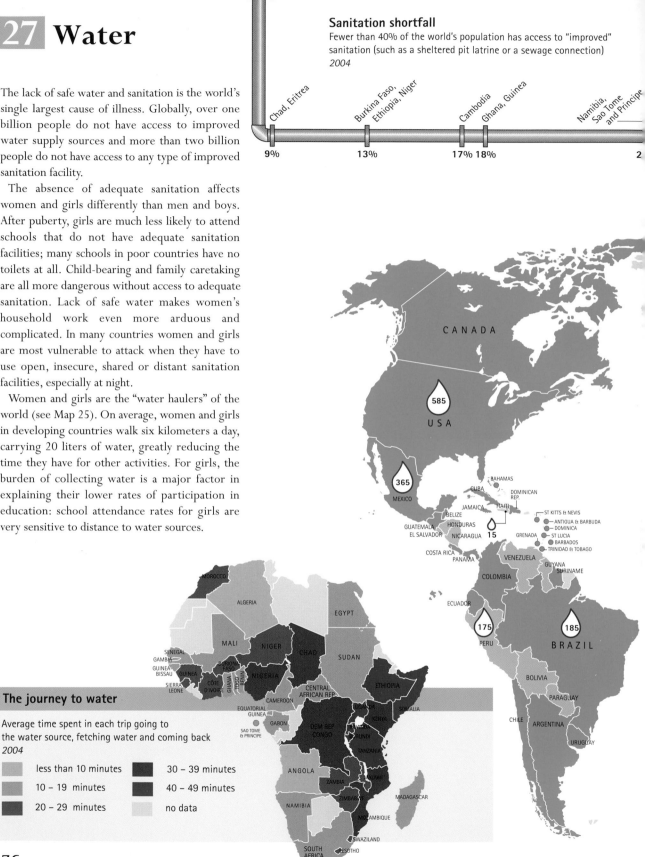

Sanitation shortfall

Fewer than 40% of the world's population has access to "improved" sanitation (such as a sheltered pit latrine or a sewage connection)
2004

Chad, Eritrea — 9%
Burkina Faso, Ethiopia, Niger — 13%
Cambodia — 17%
Ghana, Guinea — 18%
Namibia, Sao Tome and Principe — 2

The journey to water

Average time spent in each trip going to the water source, fetching water and coming back
2004

- less than 10 minutes
- 10 – 19 minutes
- 20 – 29 minutes
- 30 – 39 minutes
- 40 – 49 minutes
- no data

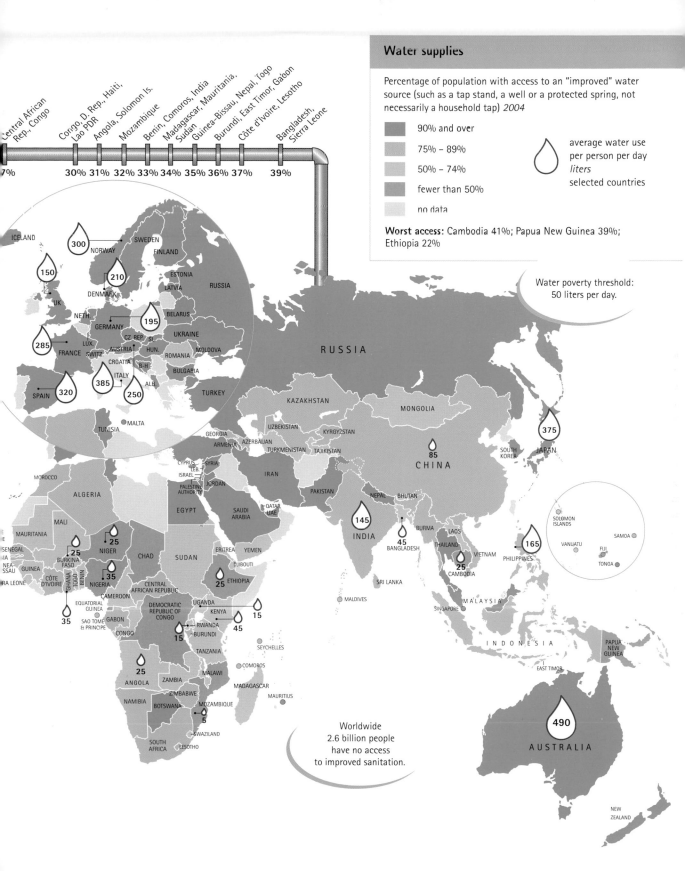

Water supplies

Percentage of population with access to an "improved" water source (such as a tap stand, a well or a protected spring, not necessarily a household tap) *2004*

- 90% and over
- 75% – 89%
- 50% – 74%
- fewer than 50%
- no data

average water use per person per day *liters* selected countries

Worst access: Cambodia 41%; Papua New Guinea 39%; Ethiopia 22%

Central African Rep., Congo — 7%
Corgo, D. Rep., Haiti, Lao PDR — 30%
Angola, Solomon Is. — 31%
Mozambique — 32%
Benin, Comoros, India — 33%
Madagascar, Mauritania, Sudan — 34%
Guinea-Bissau, Nepal, Togo — 35%
Burundi, East Timor, Gabon — 36%
Côte d'Ivoire, Lesotho — 37%
Bangladesh, Sierra Leone — 39%

Water poverty threshold: 50 liters per day.

Worldwide 2.6 billion people have no access to improved sanitation.

ICELAND — 150
NORWAY — 300
SWEDEN
FINLAND
DENMARK — 210
GERMANY — 195
UK — 285
FRANCE
SPAIN — 320
ITALY — 385
250
RUSSIA
ESTONIA
LATVIA
BELARUS
UKRAINE
NETH.
LUX
SWITZ.
CZ. REP.
AUSTRIA
SL.
HUN.
CROATIA
B-H
ROMANIA
MOLDOVA
BULGARIA
ALB.
TURKEY
TUNISIA
MALTA
GEORGIA
ARMENIA
AZERBAIJAN
KAZAKHSTAN
UZBEKISTAN
TURKMENISTAN
KYRGYZSTAN
TAJIKISTAN
MONGOLIA
CHINA — 85
SOUTH KOREA
JAPAN — 375
MOROCCO
ALGERIA
CYPRUS
LEB.
ISRAEL
SYRIA
JORDAN
PALESTINE AUTHORITY
IRAN
PAKISTAN
NEPAL — 45
BHUTAN
INDIA — 145
BANGLADESH
BURMA
LAOS
THAILAND
VIETNAM
CAMBODIA — 25
PHILIPPINES — 165
MALI
MAURITANIA
SENEGAL
NEA-SSAU
GUINEA
RA LEONE
CÔTE D'IVOIRE
GHANA
TOGO
BENIN
BURKINA FASO — 25
NIGER — 25
NIGERIA — 35
CHAD
SUDAN
EGYPT
SAUDI ARABIA
QATAR
UAE
YEMEN
ERITREA
DJIBOUTI
ETHIOPIA — 25
CENTRAL AFRICAN REPUBLIC
UGANDA
KENYA — 45
15
CAMEROON
EQUATORIAL GUINEA — 35
GABON
SAO TOME & PRINCIPE
CONGO
DEMOCRATIC REPUBLIC OF CONGO
RWANDA
BURUNDI — 15
TANZANIA
SEYCHELLES
COMOROS
MALAWI
MADAGASCAR
MAURITIUS
ANGOLA — 25
ZAMBIA
ZIMBABWE
MOZAMBIQUE — 5
NAMIBIA
BOTSWANA
SWAZILAND
SOUTH AFRICA
LESOTHO
MALDIVES
SRI LANKA
SINGAPORE
MALAYSIA
INDONESIA
SOLOMON ISLANDS
VANUATU
FIJI
TONGA
SAMOA
EAST TIMOR
PAPUA NEW GUINEA
AUSTRALIA — 490
NEW ZEALAND

Nearly a billion people in the world are illiterate, about two-thirds of whom are women.

Generalized illiteracy is mostly a function of poverty and limited educational opportunity. Higher rates of illiteracy for women, however, also suggest entrenched gender discrimination. Some of the gender-specific factors that produce high rates of women's illiteracy include: the time overburdening of women, especially in rural areas (Map 24); the restriction of girls and women to the domestic sphere; and resistance from men who fear losing their domestic power if women become literate. Illiteracy diminishes women's economic well-being, increases their dependency on men, reinforces their ties to the domestic sphere, and diminishes their ability to control or understand their own property, wealth, health, and legal rights.

The good news is that worldwide illiteracy rates have been steadily declining over the past three decades, largely the result of efforts to increase basic educational opportunities for girls.

Global figures on illiteracy generally do not incorporate information on "functional illiteracy," which is actually growing in many of the world's richest countries. In these countries, the literacy pattern is reversed – women tend to have lower rates of functional illiteracy than men. This reflects the growing "feminization" of education (Map 30) in the post-industrial rich world.

Functional illiteracy in the USA

Percentage of adults in the USA
below basic competence
2003

🔲 women
🔲 men

	quantitative literacy	prose literacy	document literacy
women	22	12	11
men	21	15	14

CANADA

USA

MEXICO

BAHAMAS

CUBA

JAMAICA

HAITI

DOMINICAN REP.

GUATEMALA
EL SALVADOR

HONDURAS

NICARAGUA

BARBADOS

TRINIDAD & TOBAGO

COSTA RICA

PANAMA

VENEZUELA

GUYANA

SURINAME

COLOMBIA

ECUADOR

PERU

BRAZIL

BOLIVIA

PARAGUAY

CHILE

ARGENTINA

URUGUAY

Gender difference in maths and literacy

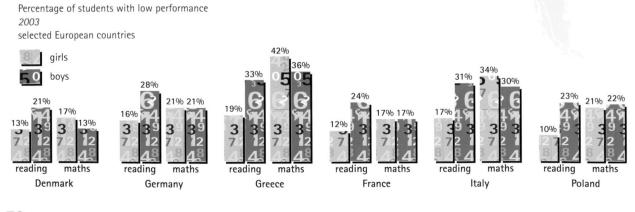

Percentage of students with low performance
2003
selected European countries

🔲 girls
🔲 boys

	reading	maths		reading	maths		reading	maths		reading	maths		reading	maths		reading	maths
	13%	21%	17%	13%	16%	28%	21%	21%	19%	42%	36%		12%	24%	17%	17%	17%	31%	34%	30%	10%	23%	21%	22%

Denmark	Germany	Greece	France	Italy	Poland

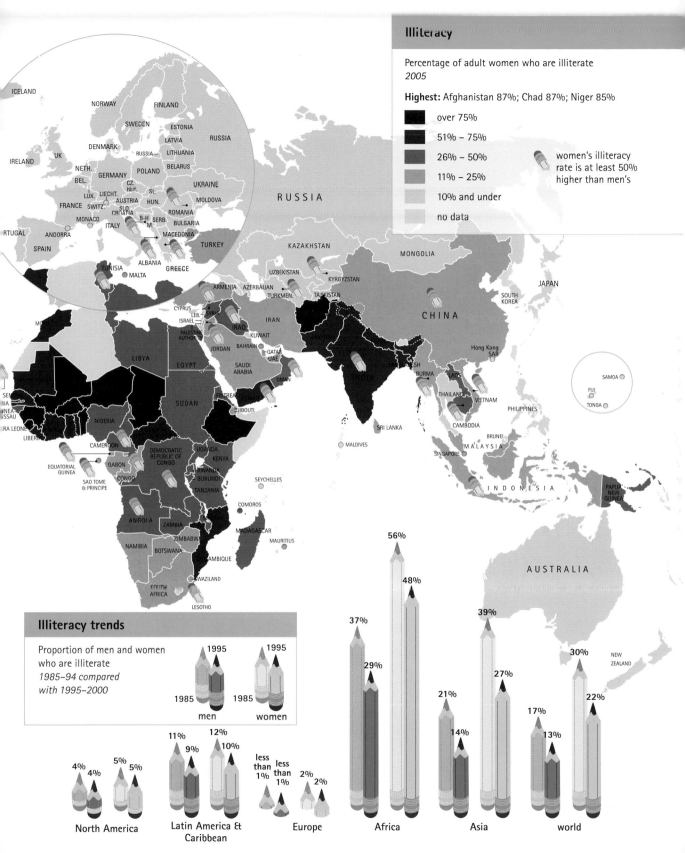

Illiteracy

Percentage of adult women who are illiterate
2005

Highest: Afghanistan 87%; Chad 87%; Niger 85%

- over 75%
- 51% – 75%
- 26% – 50%
- 11% – 25%
- 10% and under
- no data

women's illiteracy rate is at least 50% higher than men's

Illiteracy trends

Proportion of men and women who are illiterate
1985–94 compared with 1995–2000

1995 / 1985 — men
1995 / 1985 — women

North America: 4% 4% / 5% 5%

Latin America & Caribbean: 11% 9% / 12% 10%

Europe: less than 1% / less than 1% / 2% 2%

Africa: 37% 29% / 56% 48%

Asia: 21% 14% / 39% 27%

world: 17% 13% / 30% 22%

79

More girls are in primary school than ever before, and more of them are staying in school longer. In many parts of the world, boy and girl primary school enrolments are now equal or almost equal. This significant advance in girls' education is the result of concerted international and national efforts to remove restrictive legislation, to enforce equally any existing mandatory-schooling legislation, and to educate parents about the importance of educating girls.

However, it is still the case that proportionally fewer girls are enrolled in school than boys, and they are removed from school at an earlier age. Girls are still held back by presumptions that educating them will be a "waste," that they should be primarily in the home not in the workplace, and that girls are less capable than boys. The biggest gaps between boy and girl enrolment rates are found in Sub-Saharan Africa. In several countries, the average number of years of total schooling for girls remains below one full year.

Despite the generally positive global trends, progress made in girls' school enrolment has proved tenuous. Girls' enrolment rates have declined in the past decade in several countries where war, economic hardship, and declining international donor assistance makes their education seem a luxury that cannot be afforded in hard times.

There are just 80 girls or fewer for every 100 boys starting school in Afghanistan, Central African Republic, Chad, Niger, Pakistan, Somalia, and Yemen.

Secondary schooling
2005

fewer than 49% of students enrolled in secondary schools are girls

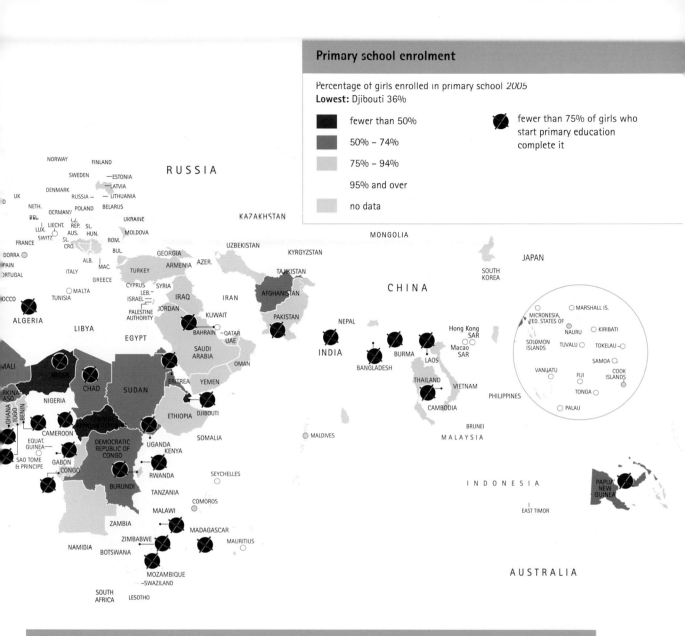

Primary school enrolment

Percentage of girls enrolled in primary school 2005
Lowest: Djibouti 36%

- fewer than 50%
- 50% – 74%
- 75% – 94%
- 95% and over
- no data

fewer than 75% of girls who start primary education complete it

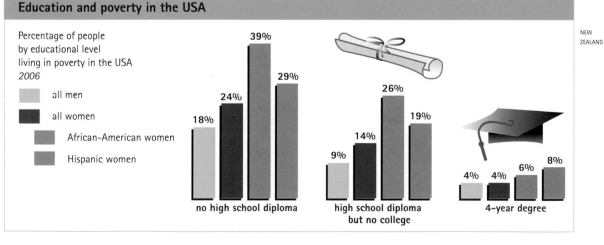

Education and poverty in the USA

Percentage of people by educational level living in poverty in the USA 2006

- all men
- all women
- African-American women
- Hispanic women

no high school diploma
18% 24% 39% 29%

high school diploma but no college
9% 14% 26% 19%

4-year degree
4% 4% 6% 8%

Worldwide, more and more women are going on to higher education, although in most countries it is still a preserve of the elite. In many industrialized countries, women now represent a slight majority of all university students. Ironically, as this trend has been identified it has immediately been labeled as worrisome: social analysts are starting to warn against the "feminization of education" and the apparent alienation of men from schooling. The proportional representation of women in university faculties has not increased at a concomitant pace.

There continue to be significant gender differences in the subjects studied and degrees taken. Women remain dramatically under represented among students and faculty in the sciences, and in technology and engineering.

Universities started to admit women in the late 19th century, often after vociferous resistance. In many countries, the gates did not open to women until the 1950s or 1960s. At most of the world's most prestigious universities there were large gaps between when they were founded and when women were admitted: 711 years at Oxford, 589 years at Cambridge, 258 years at Harvard.

University attendance is not always the most important tertiary schooling. In many countries, other third level institutions such as teachers' colleges offer the most important educational opportunities to women.

More women than men graduates in the USA
Percentages completing a four-year Bachelor's degree
2006
by race and gender

- White women 32%
- White men 25%
- Black women 22%
- Black men 15%
- Hispanic women 13%
- Hispanic men 7%

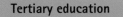

Tertiary education

Women enrolled in tertiary education as a percentage of all women
1999–2005
by region

- 1999
- 2005

Region	1999	2005
world	18%	25%
Arab states	16%	21%
Central & Eastern Europe	43%	63%
Central Asia	18%	28%
East Asia & Pacific	11%	23%
Latin America & Caribbean	23%	32%
North America & Western Europe	68%	80%
Sub-Saharan Africa	3%	4%

University

Women as a percentage of all students
2005

Highest: Saint Lucia 80%
Lowest: Eritrea 12%

60% and over

40% – 59%   under 20%

20% – 39%   no data

26%–49%

27% Namibia, Kuwait
29% Austria, Oman
31% Laos, Madagascar, S. Korea
32% Algeria, Macao (China),
    Malawi, Qatar, Switzerland,
    Tajikistan
33% Saudi Arabia, Slovenia,
    Trinidad and Tobago
34% Colombia, El Salvador,
    Germany, Italy
35% Iraq, Netherlands
36% Greece, Swaziland
37% Botswana, Croatia, Lebanon,
    Norway
38% Honduras, Turkey, Uzbekistan
39% Brunei, France, Hungary,
    Indonesia, Ireland, Spain
40% Czech Rep., India, Tunisia,
    Vietnam, UK
41% Albania, Bahrain, Belgium,
    Cape Verde, Dominican Rep.,
    Poland
42% Azerbaijan, Cyprus, Portugal,
    Slovakia
43% China, Romania, Sweden, USA
44% Brazil , Guyana, Macedonia
45% Aruba, Bulgaria, Iceland
46% Armenia, Finland, Georgia,
    Nicaragua
47% Andorra, Malaysia, Panama
48% Saint Lucia
49% Belize, Estonia

3%–25%

3% Chad
4% Guinea, Mauritania
6% Burkina Faso, Niger
10% Ethiopia
11% Ghana
12% Afghanistan, Rwanda
14% Burundi, Eritrea
15% Bangladesh,
    Comoros, Palestine
    Authority
16% Cambodia, Gambia,
    Yemen
17% Nigera, Japan,
    Pakistan
19% Iran, Uganda
21% Djibouti, Jordan,
    Mozambique
23% Malta
24% Morocco

50% and over

50% Argentina, New Zealand,
    South Africa
51% Marshall Islands, Thailand
53% Lithuania
54% Anguilla, Moldova,
    Kyrgyzstan, Russia
55% Latvia, Mongolia, British
    Virgin Islands
56% Belarus, Philippines
59% Cuba
60% Jamaica
61% Kazakhstan
67% Maldives

Women teaching
at tertiary level

As a percentage of all staff
2005

83

31 Wired Women

The internet is a powerful agent of social change, but only a small percentage of the world's people have access to it. The "digital divide" is found locally and globally – along race, class, age and gender lines. More than 80 percent of internet users are in the industrialized countries; Africa is the least wired.

Most of the world's internet users are male, higher-income, and urban. However, where the technology is most widely diffused, the gender gap is rapidly closing. Women often first learn skills and gain access to the internet in the workplace.

The internet offers great potential as a tool of political liberation. Women's groups have been fast to adopt the technology; women's websites proliferate. Unfortunately, it also offers new venues for sexual exploitation. Pornography flourishes online, and it has facilitated global trafficking (see Map 19) in women and children.

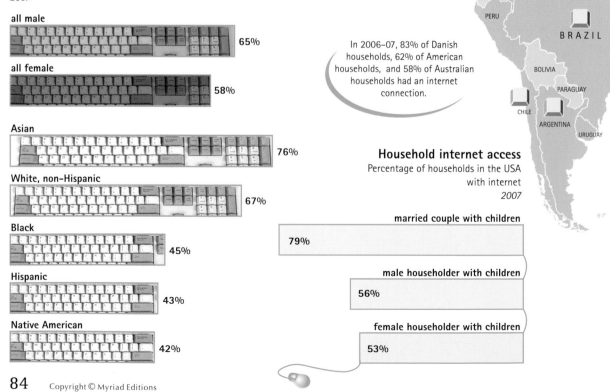

USA and Canada
Women comprise 56% of people who use Amazon.com, 51% of Yahoo users, and 47% of eBay users.

In 2006–07, 83% of Danish households, 62% of American households, and 58% of Australian households had an internet connection.

Race and gender online in the USA
Percentage of people who use internet at home
2007

all male
65%

all female
58%

Asian
76%

White, non-Hispanic
67%

Black
45%

Hispanic
43%

Native American
42%

Household internet access
Percentage of households in the USA with internet
2007

married couple with children
79%

male householder with children
56%

female householder with children
53%

84

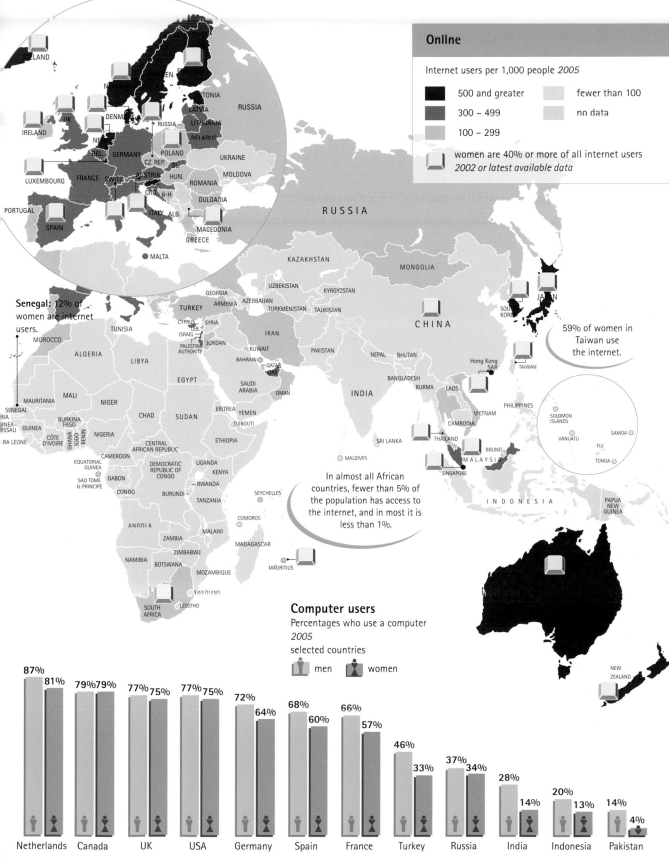

Internet users per 1,000 people *2005*

- 500 and greater
- 300 – 499
- 100 – 299
- fewer than 100
- no data

women are 40% or more of all internet users
2002 or latest available data

Senegal: 12% of women are internet users.

59% of women in Taiwan use the internet.

In almost all African countries, fewer than 5% of the population has access to the internet, and in most it is less than 1%.

Computer users

Percentages who use a computer
2005
selected countries

men   women

Country	men	women
Netherlands	87%	81%
Canada	79%	79%
UK	77%	75%
USA	77%	75%
Germany	72%	64%
Spain	68%	60%
France	66%	57%
Turkey	46%	33%
Russia	37%	34%
India	28%	14%
Indonesia	20%	13%
Pakistan	14%	4%

85

32 Property

The majority of the world's women do not equally own, inherit, or control property, land and wealth. Discriminatory legal inheritance and property ownership laws are still widely in effect around the world.

Property discrimination in agrarian economies is particularly striking – women typically work the fields, prepare, grow and harvest the food (see Map 24), but cannot own the land. Land and property provide leverage for other economic advantages. For example, land is typically required as collateral for loans; if women do not own or control land, they cannot get credit.

In industrialized countries, there is a similar pecking order for homeownership, with fewer women than men owning homes. In most industrialized countries as recently as the mid-1970s gender-based discrimination in mortgages, credit, and loans was entirely legal and widely entrenched.

Even where there is no legal discrimination, women are subject to social pressures or economic realities that create unequal access to land, property and wealth. For example, they are pressured to turn over property or financial matters to male relatives, they are pressured not to exercise their full inheritance rights, and they are socialized to believe that financial matters are beyond their realm.

Globalization has tended to deepen women's property disadvantage as the cash economy has displaced communal or household-based land use.

Home ownership in the USA

Percentage of households who own their own homes
2005

USA average: 69%

76%	61%	52%	50%
White-American	Asian-American	African-American	Hispanic-American

all households

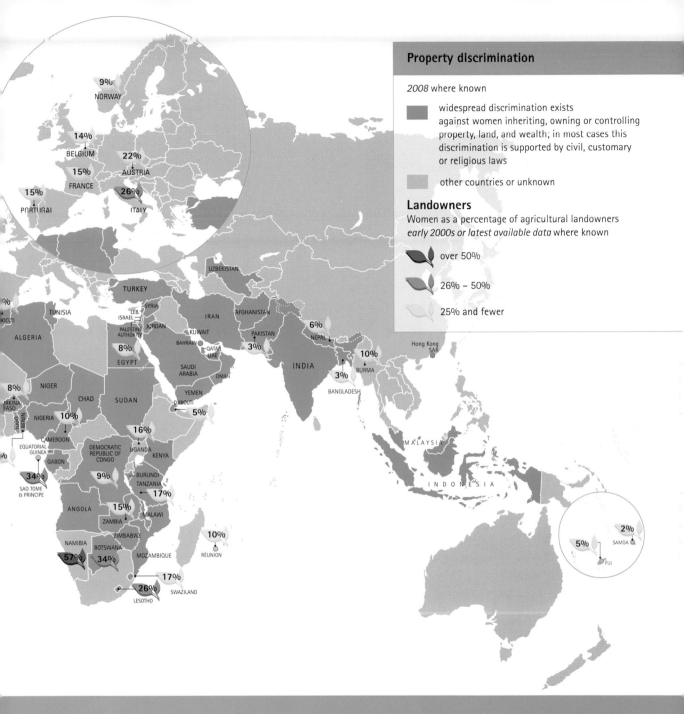

Property discrimination

2008 where known

- widespread discrimination exists against women inheriting, owning or controlling property, land, and wealth; in most cases this discrimination is supported by civil, customary or religious laws
- other countries or unknown

Landowners

Women as a percentage of agricultural landowners
early 2000s or latest available data where known

- over 50%
- 26% – 50%
- 25% and fewer

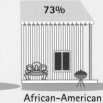
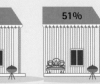

84% all races   73% African-American   63% Hispanic-American

married-couple households

50% male-headed   51% female-headed

single-parent households

50% men   59% women

single-person households

The majority of the world's population is poor. Women are the majority of the world's poor. The poorest of the poor are women. More so than men, women lack the resources either to stave off poverty in the first place, or to climb out of poverty – they have limited ownership of income, property, and credit. Women not only bear the brunt of poverty, they bear the brunt of "managing" poverty: as providers and caretakers of their families, it is women's labor and women's personal austerity that typically compensate for diminished resources of the family or household.

Official poverty rates underestimate actual deprivation, and "poverty" is hard to measure. What is clear, though, is that since the early 1990s the gulf between rich and poor has widened dramatically on scales from the global to the local. The total income of the richest one percent of the people in the world is now about the same as the total income of the poorest 60 percent.

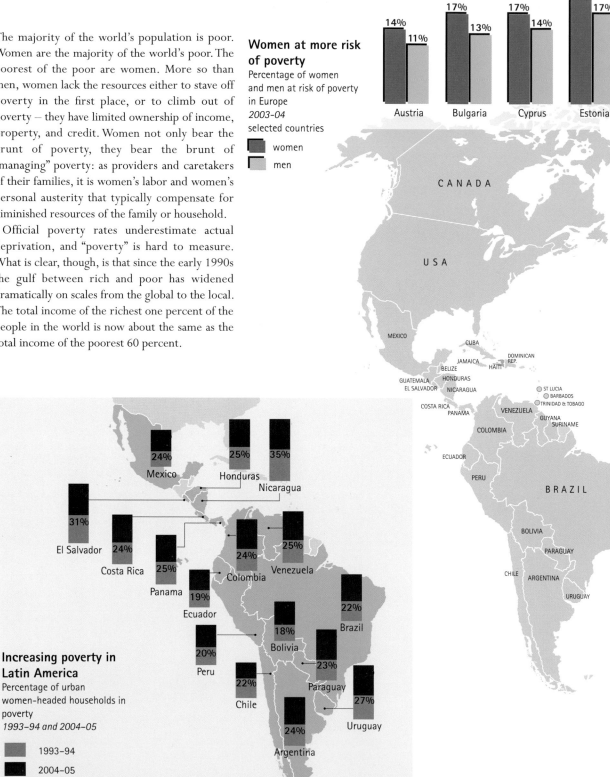

Women at more risk of poverty
Percentage of women and men at risk of poverty in Europe
2003-04
selected countries

- women
- men

Austria 14% / 11%
Bulgaria 17% / 13%
Cyprus 17% / 14%
Estonia 20% / 17%

Increasing poverty in Latin America
Percentage of urban women-headed households in poverty
1993–94 and 2004–05

- 1993–94
- 2004–05

Mexico 24%
Honduras 25%
Nicaragua 35%
El Salvador 31%
Costa Rica 24%
Panama 25%
Colombia 24%
Venezuela 25%
Ecuador 19%
Bolivia 18%
Brazil 22%
Peru 20%
Paraguay 23%
Chile 22%
Uruguay 27%
Argentina 24%

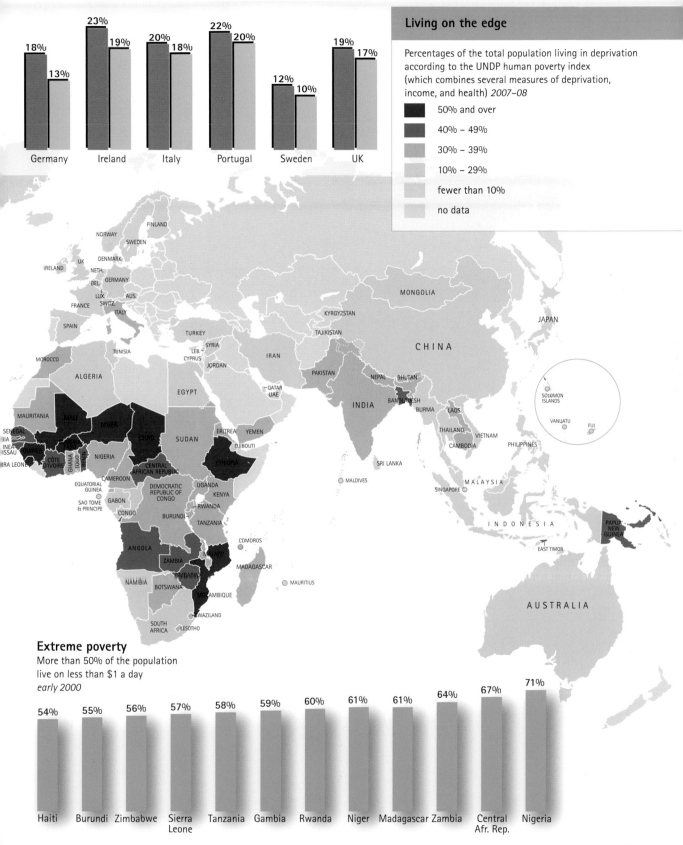

Living on the edge

Percentages of the total population living in deprivation according to the UNDP human poverty index (which combines several measures of deprivation, income, and health) *2007–08*

- 50% and over
- 40% – 49%
- 30% – 39%
- 10% – 29%
- fewer than 10%
- no data

Germany 18% / 13%
Ireland 23% / 19%
Italy 20% / 18%
Portugal 22% / 20%
Sweden 12% / 10%
UK 19% / 17%

Extreme poverty
More than 50% of the population live on less than $1 a day
early 2000

Haiti 54%
Burundi 55%
Zimbabwe 56%
Sierra Leone 57%
Tanzania 58%
Gambia 59%
Rwanda 60%
Niger 61%
Madagascar 61%
Zambia 64%
Central Afr. Rep. 67%
Nigeria 71%

Women are the "shock-absorbers" of economic crises. When governments cut back spending on social and health services to cope with their debt burden, poor households, of which women-headed households are a disproportionate share, bear the brunt of these cuts. Women's labor keeps households going.

Economic adjustment programs imposed by the International Monetary Fund (IMF) and World Bank on governments in exchange for loans have deepened poverty and increased social inequities. Most Eastern European, African and Latin American governments are now heavily in debt. Under great pressure from critics, the World Bank has now started to develop "poverty alleviation" programs. Critics say it is too little, too late.

Poverty versus power
2008
- 70% of the world's poor are women
- 8% of the executive directors of the World Bank are women
- 4% of the executive directors and none of the managing directors of the International Monetary Fund are women.

Regional trends

External debt as a percentage of GNI
1986, 1996, 2006

- 1986
- 1996
- 2006

Sub-Saharan Africa
54% 72% 26%

Middle East & North Africa
41% 49% 22%

South Asia
24% 29% 20%

East Asia and Pacific
29% 33% 18%

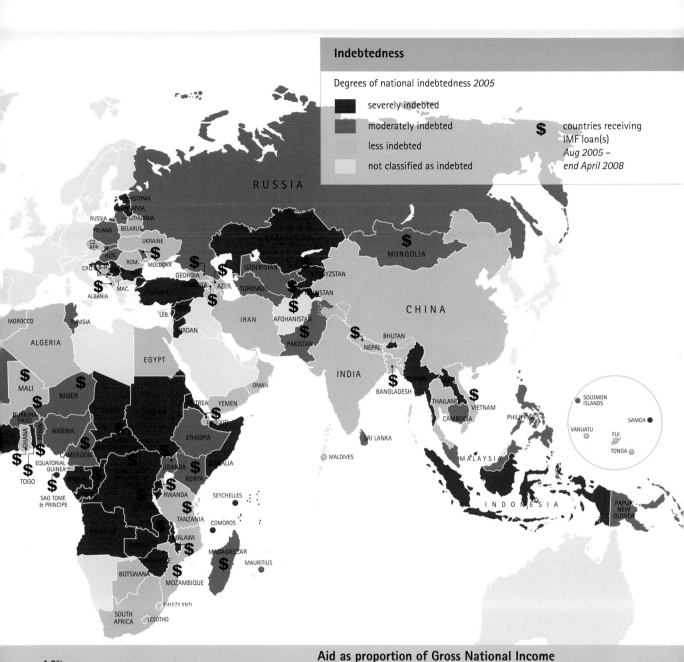

Indebtedness

Degrees of national indebtedness *2005*

- severely indebted
- moderately indebted
- less indebted
- not classified as indebted

$ countries receiving IMF loan(s) Aug 2005 – end April 2008

RUSSIA

ESTONIA
LATVIA
LITHUANIA
RUSSIA
BELARUS
POLAND
CZ.
REP. SL. UKRAINE
HUN.
ROM. MOLDOVA
CRO. B-H SER. GEORGIA
M. BUL. AZER.
MAC. ARMENIA
ALBANIA TURKEY
LEB.
JORDAN

MOROCCO
TUNISIA
ALGERIA
EGYPT

KAZAKHSTAN
MONGOLIA
UZBEKISTAN
KYRGYZSTAN
TURKMEN. TAJIKISTAN
CHINA
IRAN AFGHANISTAN
PAKISTAN
BHUTAN
NEPAL
INDIA BURMA
BANGLADESH
OMAN THAILAND VIETNAM
CAMBODIA PHILIPPINES
SRI LANKA

MALI
NIGER
BURKINA
FASO
GHANA BENIN
NIGERIA CHAD SUDAN
ERITREA YEMEN
DJIBOUTI
CAMEROON CENTRAL AFRICAN REP. ETHIOPIA
EQUATORIAL GUINEA
TOGO GABON UGANDA SOMALIA
SAO TOME DEMOCRATIC KENYA
& PRINCIPE REPUBLIC OF CONGO
RWANDA
BURUNDI SEYCHELLES
TANZANIA
COMOROS
ANGOLA MALAWI
ZAMBIA MADAGASCAR
MAURITIUS
ZIMBABWE
BOTSWANA MOZAMBIQUE
SWAZILAND
SOUTH LESOTHO
AFRICA

MALDIVES

MALAYSIA
INDONESIA
PAPUA NEW GUINEA

SOLOMON ISLANDS
SAMOA
VANUATU
FIJI
TONGA

Aid as proportion of Gross National Income

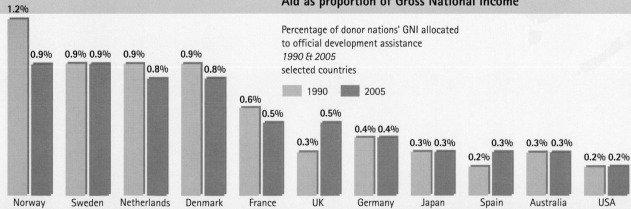

Percentage of donor nations' GNI allocated to official development assistance
1990 & 2005
selected countries

- 1990
- 2005

	Norway	Sweden	Netherlands	Denmark	France	UK	Germany	Japan	Spain	Australia	USA
1990	1.2%	0.9%	0.9%	0.9%	0.6%	0.3%	0.4%	0.3%	0.2%	0.3%	0.2%
2005	0.9%	0.9%	0.8%	0.8%	0.5%	0.5%	0.4%	0.3%	0.3%	0.3%	0.2%

91

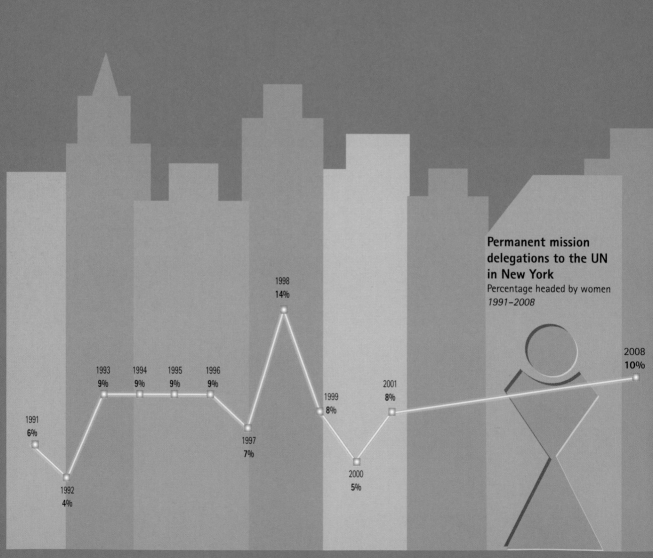

Permanent mission delegations to the UN in New York
Percentage headed by women
1991–2008

1991
6%

1992
4%

1993
9%

1994
9%

1995
9%

1996
9%

1997
7%

1998
14%

1999
8%

2000
5%

2001
8%

2008
10%

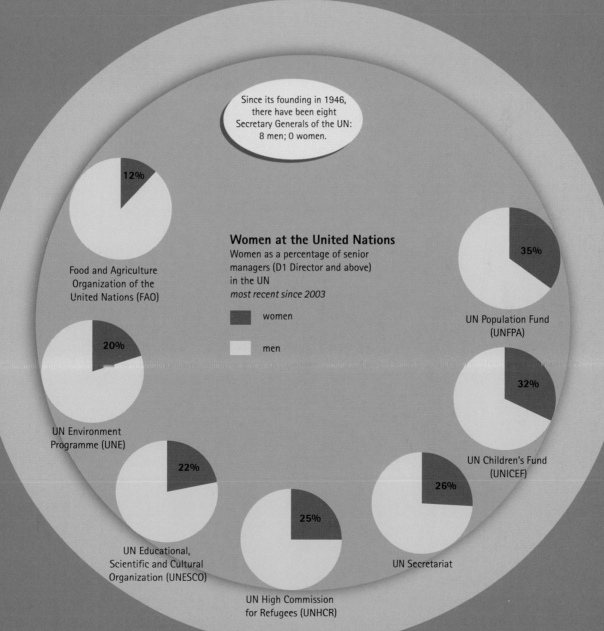

Since its founding in 1946, there have been eight Secretary Generals of the UN: 8 men; 0 women.

Women at the United Nations
Women as a percentage of senior managers (D1 Director and above) in the UN
most recent since 2003

■ women

□ men

12%
Food and Agriculture Organization of the United Nations (FAO)

20%
UN Environment Programme (UNE)

22%
UN Educational, Scientific and Cultural Organization (UNESCO)

25%
UN High Commission for Refugees (UNHCR)

26%
UN Secretariat

32%
UN Children's Fund (UNICEF)

35%
UN Population Fund (UNFPA)

In most countries, men gained the right to vote before women. Almost everywhere, voting rights for women were resisted, sometimes fiercely.

For most countries, it is difficult to identify a single date when women won the vote. This right was often doled out in stages, and restricted suffrage was common. Typically some women — such as married women, literate women, or the wives of soldiers — were granted the vote before others. In colonized countries, women of the colonizing class almost always had the vote before indigenous women.

In reality, the right to vote does not ensure the exercise of that right. Many governments restrict or entirely prevent anyone from voting.

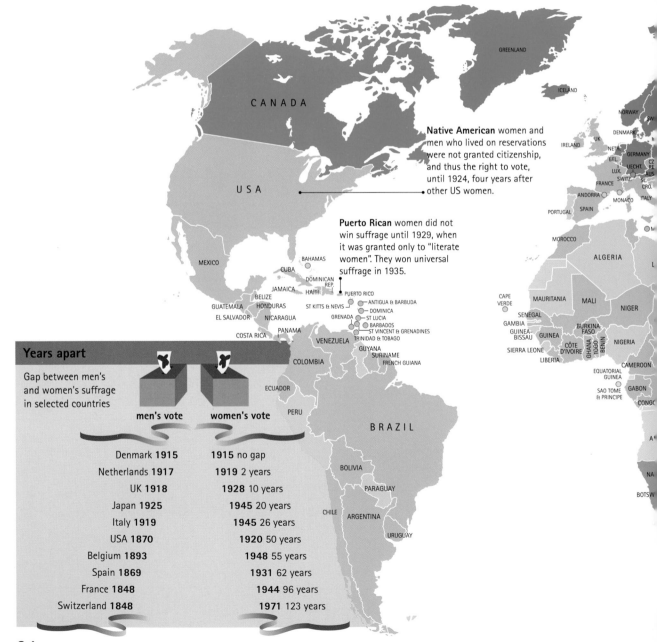

Native American women and men who lived on reservations were not granted citizenship, and thus the right to vote, until 1924, four years after other US women.

Puerto Rican women did not win suffrage until 1929, when it was granted only to "literate women". They won universal suffrage in 1935.

Years apart

Gap between men's and women's suffrage in selected countries

	men's vote	women's vote
Denmark	**1915**	**1915** no gap
Netherlands	**1917**	**1919** 2 years
UK	**1918**	**1928** 10 years
Japan	**1925**	**1945** 20 years
Italy	**1919**	**1945** 26 years
USA	**1870**	**1920** 50 years
Belgium	**1893**	**1948** 55 years
Spain	**1869**	**1931** 62 years
France	**1848**	**1944** 96 years
Switzerland	**1848**	**1971** 123 years

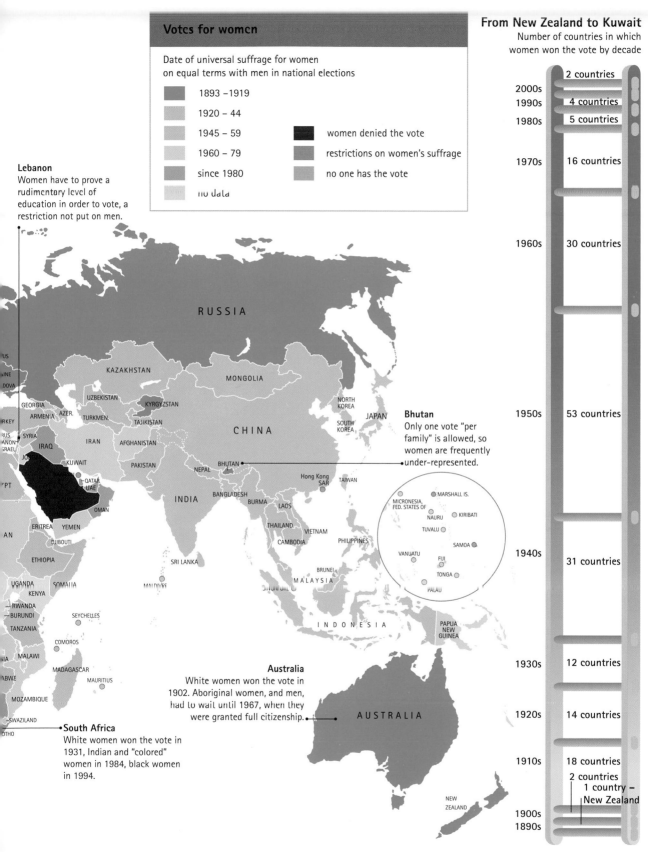

Votes for women

Date of universal suffrage for women on equal terms with men in national elections

- 1893–1919
- 1920–44
- 1945–59
- 1960–79
- since 1980
- no data
- women denied the vote
- restrictions on women's suffrage
- no one has the vote

Lebanon
Women have to prove a rudimentary level of education in order to vote, a restriction not put on men.

Bhutan
Only one vote "per family" is allowed, so women are frequently under-represented.

Australia
White women won the vote in 1902. Aboriginal women, and men, had to wait until 1967, when they were granted full citizenship.

South Africa
White women won the vote in 1931, Indian and "colored" women in 1984, black women in 1994.

From New Zealand to Kuwait
Number of countries in which women won the vote by decade

Decade	Countries
2000s	2 countries
1990s	4 countries
1980s	5 countries
1970s	16 countries
1960s	30 countries
1950s	53 countries
1940s	31 countries
1930s	12 countries
1920s	14 countries
1910s	18 countries
1900s	2 countries
1890s	1 country – New Zealand

95

This map is a snapshot of women's representation in government in 2007. A few patterns persist across time and space: nowhere do women have equal representation with men in government; in only a very few countries do women represent 25 percent or more of elected legislators; the states with the highest shares of women in elected office are those that enforce explicit policies promoting equality – most notably, countries in Scandinavia.

The world average of women in legislatures dropped dramatically between the mid-1980s and the mid-1990s, as the result of sweeping political changes in Eastern Europe and the former USSR, which resulted in a sharp drop in women's representation in government in those states.

The presence of women in government is important not only for the rights of women, but, perhaps, for the nature of governance itself. Recent studies suggest that when women are elected in sufficient numbers they introduce different perceptions of the norms of appropriate governance. In only a few states have women achieved a "critical mass" of elected representation.

In many countries, elected officials have little influence over actual governance. Authoritarian regimes abound, and other states have weak legislatures. Nonetheless, electing women even to weak legislatures can have considerable symbolic significance – as is demonstrated by the change in governance in Afghanistan between 2001 and 2002.

Women in parliament
Percentage worldwide
1945–2007

1945	1955	1965	1975	1985	1995	2005	2007
3%	7.5%	8%	11%	12%	12%	16%	17%

Grenada 40%
South Africa 41%
Norway 44%
Germany 46%
Finland 47%
Spain 50%
Sweden 52%

Paraguay 31%
Denmark 33%
Croatia 33%
Austria 35%
El Salvador 35%
Colombia 36%
Rwanda 36%
Netherlands 36%
Guinea-Bissau 38%

Costa Rica 25%
Philippines 25%
Guatemala 25%
Haiti 25%
Zambia 25%
Bahamas 27%
Botswana 27%
Iceland 27%
Lesotho 28%
UK 29%
Barbados 29%

Women in ministerial positions
Percentage where 25% and over
January 2005

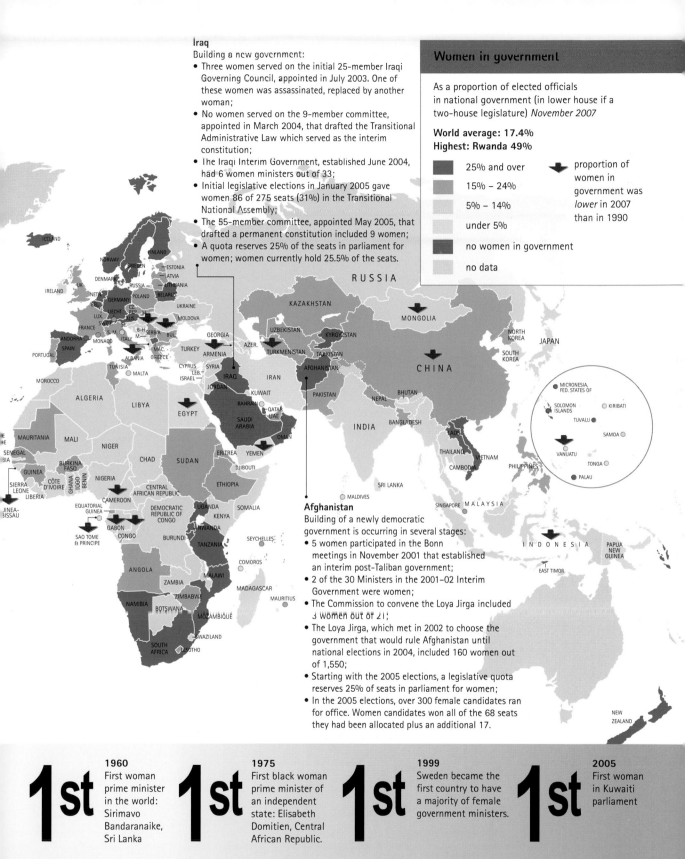

Iraq

Building a new government:

- Three women served on the initial 25-member Iraqi Governing Council, appointed in July 2003. One of these women was assassinated, replaced by another woman;
- No women served on the 9-member committee, appointed in March 2004, that drafted the Transitional Administrative Law which served as the interim constitution;
- The Iraqi Interim Government, established June 2004, had 6 women ministers out of 33;
- Initial legislative elections in January 2005 gave women 86 of 275 seats (31%) in the Transitional National Assembly;
- The 55-member committee, appointed May 2005, that drafted a permanent constitution included 9 women;
- A quota reserves 25% of the seats in parliament for women; women currently hold 25.5% of the seats.

Women in government

As a proportion of elected officials in national government (in lower house if a two-house legislature) *November 2007*

World average: 17.4%
Highest: Rwanda 49%

- 25% and over
- 15% – 24%
- 5% – 14%
- under 5%
- no women in government
- no data

proportion of women in government was *lower* in 2007 than in 1990

Afghanistan

Building of a newly democratic government is occurring in several stages:

- 5 women participated in the Bonn meetings in November 2001 that established an interim post-Taliban government;
- 2 of the 30 Ministers in the 2001–02 Interim Government were women;
- The Commission to convene the Loya Jirga included 3 women out of 21;
- The Loya Jirga, which met in 2002 to choose the government that would rule Afghanistan until national elections in 2004, included 160 women out of 1,550;
- Starting with the 2005 elections, a legislative quota reserves 25% of seats in parliament for women;
- In the 2005 elections, over 300 female candidates ran for office. Women candidates won all of the 68 seats they had been allocated plus an additional 17.

1st
1960
First woman prime minister in the world: Sirimavo Bandaranaike, Sri Lanka

1st
1975
First black woman prime minister of an independent state: Elisabeth Domitien, Central African Republic.

1st
1999
Sweden became the first country to have a majority of female government ministers.

1st
2005
First woman in Kuwaiti parliament

37 Seats of Power

Almost everywhere in the world women are now at least visible in national legislatures. An increasing number of countries and political parties have passed legislation to ensure this. In 2008 quota or reservation systems existed in more than 25 countries, although they are controversial, perhaps no more so than among women themselves.

Around the world, increasing numbers of women are active in local governance, in city councils and in mayoralties.

The ranks of heads of national government, though, remain resolutely male dominated. Fewer than 50 countries have ever had a woman head of government, and some of those were in short-term caretaker positions. Women who hold ceremonial or "head of state" positions are not included on this map.

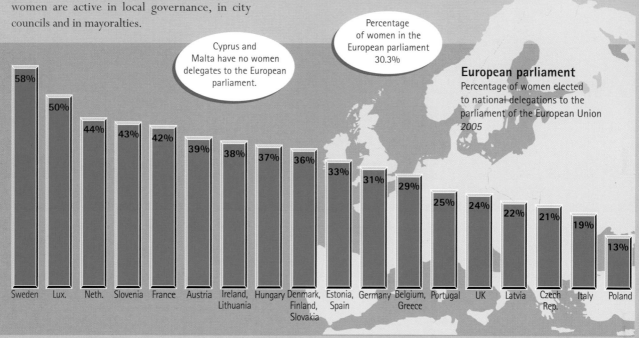

Cyprus and Malta have no women delegates to the European parliament.

Percentage of women in the European parliament 30.3%

European parliament
Percentage of women elected to national delegations to the parliament of the European Union 2005

58% Sweden
50% Lux.
44% Neth.
43% Slovenia
42% France
39% Austria
38% Ireland, Lithuania
37% Hungary
36% Denmark, Finland, Slovakia
33% Estonia, Spain
31% Germany
29% Belgium, Greece
25% Portugal
24% UK
22% Latvia
21% Czech Rep.
19% Italy
13% Poland

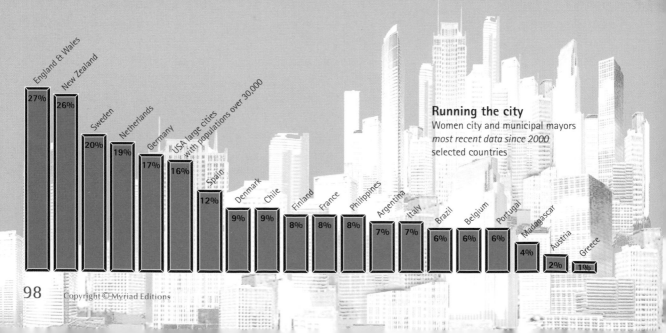

Running the city
Women city and municipal mayors
most recent data since 2000
selected countries

27% England & Wales
26% New Zealand
20% Sweden
19% Netherlands
17% Germany
16% USA large cities with populations over 30,000
12% Spain
9% Denmark
9% Chile
8% Finland
8% France
8% Philippines
7% Argentina
7% Italy
6% Brazil
6% Belgium
6% Portugal
4% Madagascar
2% Austria
1% Greece

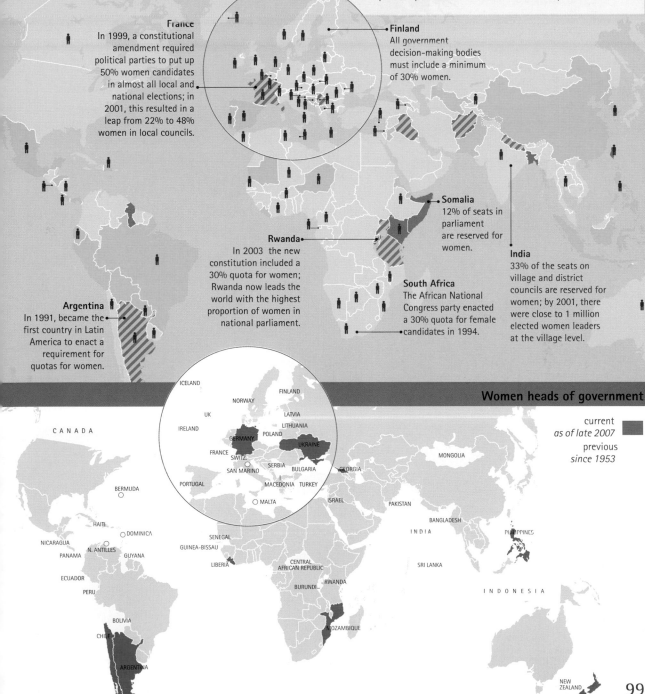

Quotas for national parliament

2007

The 1995 "Platform for Action" from the UN Beijing conference called on governments to ensure "women's equal access to and full participation in power structures and decision making". Quotas are one route to this goal, although they are controversial and their success is mixed.

established through the constitution

established through election laws

 political parties have their own candidate quotas

France
In 1999, a constitutional amendment required political parties to put up 50% women candidates in almost all local and national elections; in 2001, this resulted in a leap from 22% to 48% women in local councils.

Finland
All government decision-making bodies must include a minimum of 30% women.

Rwanda
In 2003 the new constitution included a 30% quota for women; Rwanda now leads the world with the highest proportion of women in national parliament.

Somalia
12% of seats in parliament are reserved for women.

South Africa
The African National Congress party enacted a 30% quota for female candidates in 1994.

India
33% of the seats on village and district councils are reserved for women; by 2001, there were close to 1 million elected women leaders at the village level.

Argentina
In 1991, became the first country in Latin America to enact a requirement for quotas for women.

Women heads of government

current
as of late 2007
previous
since 1953

ICELAND
NORWAY
FINLAND
UK
LATVIA
IRELAND
LITHUANIA
GERMANY
POLAND
FRANCE
SWITZ.
UKRAINE
SAN MARINO
SERBIA
BULGARIA
GEORGIA
PORTUGAL
MACEDONIA TURKEY
MALTA

CANADA
MONGOLIA
BERMUDA
HAITI
DOMINICA
ISRAEL
PAKISTAN
NICARAGUA
N. ANTILLES
SENEGAL
BANGLADESH
PANAMA
GUYANA
GUINEA-BISSAU
INDIA
PHILIPPINES
ECUADOR
LIBERIA
CENTRAL AFRICAN REPUBLIC
SRI LANKA
PERU
BURUNDI
RWANDA
INDONESIA
BOLIVIA
MOZAMBIQUE
CHILE
ARGENTINA
NEW ZEALAND

Many regions of the world are in extreme crisis, fractured by wars, insurgencies, ethnic conflicts, famine and economic collapse. Millions of people are displaced, and struggling for survival against great odds. The global population of refugees, including internally displaced people, is estimated at between 35 and 45 million. Most armed conflicts today are civil wars, and most of these involve the deliberate targeting of civilians.

Women bear specific burdens in crisis zones. Their responsibility for sustaining families is increased, but the resources available to meet those needs are diminished. Prostitution and the trafficking of girls and women (see Map 20) increases as a result of armed insurgent strategy or civilian destitution. Wartime rape is endemic and often systematic.

Sexual offences as acts of war have been broadly proscribed since the 1940s, but it was only in the mid-1990s that feminists succeeded in having war rape specifically designated as a prosecutable war crime.

Crisis zones

2000–08

periods of major armed conflict or economic crisis

Chiapas (Mexico): internal conflict, ethnic tensions

Guatemala: internal conflict, ethnic conflicts (*vs* indigenous peoples)

Haiti: internal conflict, political upheaval, famine

Colombia: internal war/insurgencies

Peru: internal conflict/insurgencies

Guinea: war/internal insurgencies

Sierra Leone: war, internal war, massacres, ethnic cleansing

Côte d'Ivoire internal conflic

MEXICO
GUATEMALA
HAITI
COLOMBIA
ECUADOR
PERU
FRENCH GUIANA
SENEGAL
GUINEA
SIERRA LEONE
LIBERIA

Refugees

Places of refuge for major refugee populations
end 2006 or latest available data

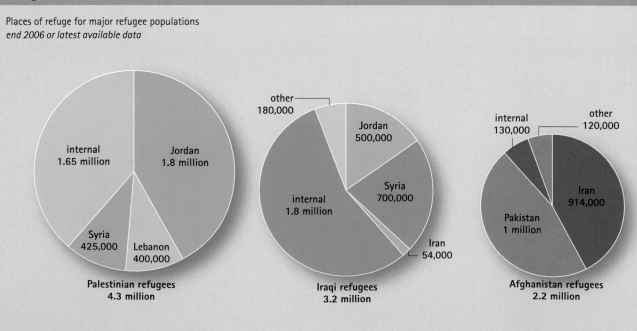

internal 1.65 million
Jordan 1.8 million
Syria 425,000
Lebanon 400,000

Palestinian refugees 4.3 million

other 180,000
Jordan 500,000
Syria 700,000
internal 1.8 million
Iran 54,000

Iraqi refugees 3.2 million

internal 130,000
other 120,000
Iran 914,000
Pakistan 1 million

Afghanistan refugees 2.2 million

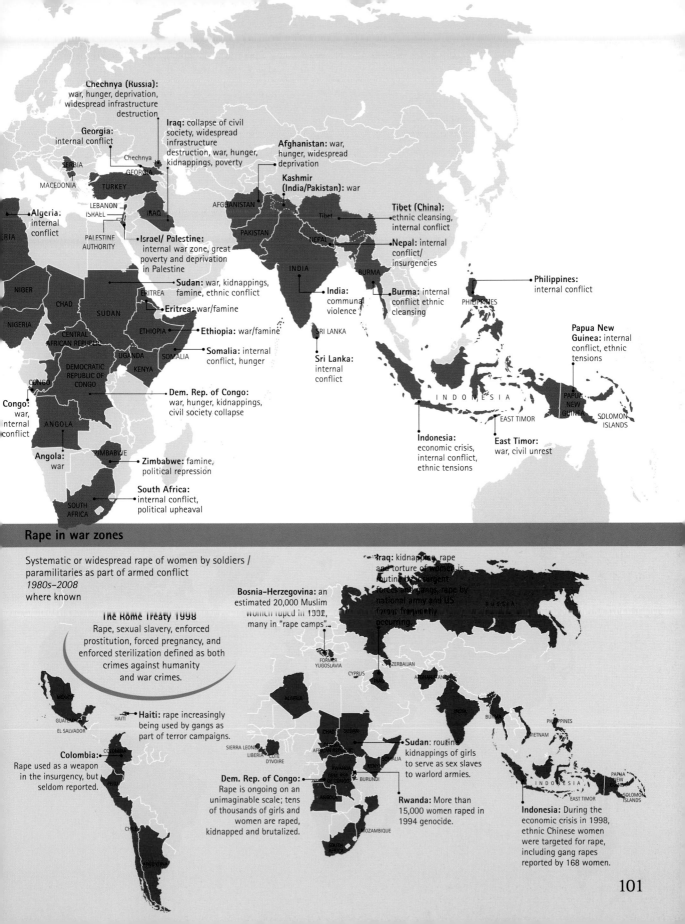

Chechnya (Russia): war, hunger, deprivation, widespread infrastructure destruction

Georgia: internal conflict

Iraq: collapse of civil society, widespread infrastructure destruction, war, hunger, kidnappings, poverty

Afghanistan: war, hunger, widespread deprivation

Kashmir (India/Pakistan): war

Tibet (China): ethnic cleansing, internal conflict

Nepal: internal conflict/ insurgencies

Philippines: internal conflict

Algeria: internal conflict

Israel/ Palestine: internal war zone, great poverty and deprivation in Palestine

Sudan: war, kidnappings, famine, ethnic conflict

Eritrea: war/famine

Ethiopia: war/famine

India: communal violence

Burma: internal conflict ethnic cleansing

Papua New Guinea: internal conflict, ethnic tensions

Somalia: internal conflict, hunger

Sri Lanka: internal conflict

Dem. Rep. of Congo: war, hunger, kidnappings, civil society collapse

Congo: war, internal conflict

Angola: war

Zimbabwe: famine, political repression

Indonesia: economic crisis, internal conflict, ethnic tensions

East Timor: war, civil unrest

South Africa: internal conflict, political upheaval

Rape in war zones

Systematic or widespread rape of women by soldiers / paramilitaries as part of armed conflict
1980s–2008
where known

The Rome Treaty 1998
Rape, sexual slavery, enforced prostitution, forced pregnancy, and enforced sterilization defined as both crimes against humanity and war crimes.

Iraq: kidnapping, rape and torture of women is routine by insurgent forces and gangs, rape by national army and US forces frequently occurring

Bosnia–Herzegovina: an estimated 20,000 Muslim women raped in 1992, many in "rape camps".

Haiti: rape increasingly being used by gangs as part of terror campaigns.

Colombia: Rape used as a weapon in the insurgency, but seldom reported.

Dem. Rep. of Congo: Rape is ongoing on an unimaginable scale; tens of thousands of girls and women are raped, kidnapped and brutalized.

Sudan: routine kidnappings of girls to serve as sex slaves to warlord armies.

Rwanda: More than 15,000 women raped in 1994 genocide.

Indonesia: During the economic crisis in 1998, ethnic Chinese women were targeted for rape, including gang rapes reported by 168 women.

101

Military service is traditionally the preserve of men – and they have fought hard to keep it that way. Contested constructions of femininity and masculinity shape the debates about whether women should participate in militaries. Militaries have been imagined as proving grounds for masculinity; allowing women in challenges ideals of both male and female behaviour. Military strategists also argue that the presence of women interferes with the male bonding essential to military "readiness." Similar arguments have been raised against gays and lesbians serving in militaries.

Among feminists, too, women's participation in militaries is controversial. On the one hand, militaries provide employment opportunities, and military service is represented as the pinnacle of service to the nation. On the other hand, it is argued that women's participation in masculinized institutions of organized violence harms the long-term interests of all women.

Active duty
Number of women generals
2006

1	2	2	3	47
Netherlands	Romania	UK	Canada	USA

Restrictions on women's participation

2007 where known

● restrictions exist
women excluded from holding certain military posts

○ no restrictions
women can serve in all military positions

Firts

USA 1993
US lifts the Air Force ban on women flying combat missions

UK 1995, Taiwan 1996
First women pilots certified to fly combat airplanes.

Israel 1995
Supreme Court rules women must be allowed to train as combat pilots.

Norway 1995
World's first woman submarine commander.

Brazil 1995, Argentina 1996 Austria 1998, Italy 2000
Women allowed to serve in active duty forces for the first time.

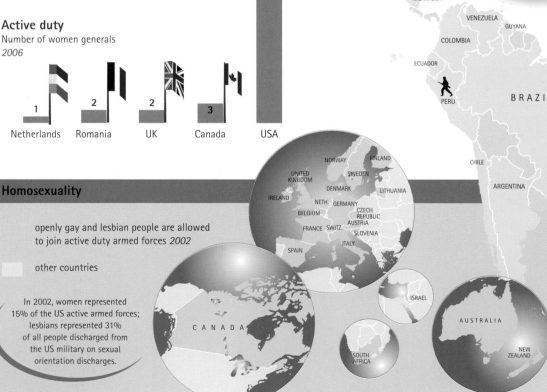

Homosexuality

openly gay and lesbian people are allowed to join active duty armed forces *2002*

other countries

In 2002, women represented 15% of the US active armed forces; lesbians represented 31% of all people discharged from the US military on sexual orientation discharges.

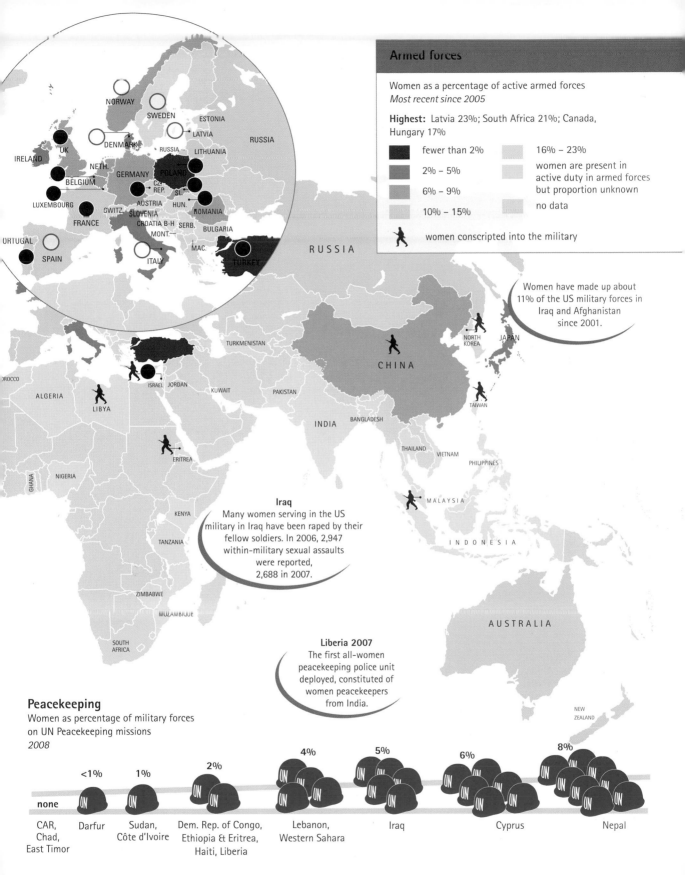

Armed forces

Women as a percentage of active armed forces
Most recent since 2005

Highest: Latvia 23%; South Africa 21%; Canada, Hungary 17%

fewer than 2%	16% – 23%
2% – 5%	women are present in active duty in armed forces but proportion unknown
6% – 9%	
10% – 15%	no data

women conscripted into the military

Women have made up about 11% of the US military forces in Iraq and Afghanistan since 2001.

Iraq
Many women serving in the US military in Iraq have been raped by their fellow soldiers. In 2006, 2,947 within-military sexual assaults were reported, 2,688 in 2007.

Liberia 2007
The first all-women peacekeeping police unit deployed, constituted of women peacekeepers from India.

Peacekeeping
Women as percentage of military forces on UN Peacekeeping missions
2008

none	<1%	1%	2%	4%	5%	6%	8%
CAR, Chad, East Timor	Darfur	Sudan, Côte d'Ivoire	Dem. Rep. of Congo, Ethiopia & Eritrea, Haiti, Liberia	Lebanon, Western Sahara	Iraq	Cyprus	Nepal

103

40 Feminisms

Scotland 2002: Members of Scottish Episcopal Church in Edinburgh vote in favor of law allowing women to become bishops.

UK 2001: The "morning-after" contraceptive pill becomes available without a prescription for women over the age of 16.

Norway 2002: Government orders companies to ensure that at least 40% of their board members are women. State-owned firms have just 12 months to comply, the 650 public companies have up to 3 years. If they fail to meet the deadlines, the government will bring in legislation to enforce the quotas.

Netherlands 2001: Gay and lesbian marriages granted full recognition on equal terms with heterosexual marriages.

Spain 2008: Spanish Prime Minister appoints a majority-women cabinet, including Spain's first woman Defense Minister.

USA
2000: Government approves use of RU486, a non-surgical abortifacent.
1996: Government directive officially prohibits US military personnel from engaging in child prostitution. The directive states that "any use of child prostitutes is an egregious exploitation of children... and...is detrimental to the health and welfare of service members and the ability of the US forces to carry out their mission."

Colombia
2002: About 20,000 women participate in a women's peace march in Bogota to demand the end to the civil war, many shouting "We won't give birth to more sons to send to war."
2001: The Mayor of Bogota calls for a one-night curfew on all men, forbidding them to be out in the city streets for a night in order to draw attention to epidemic rates of violence against women.

Brazil 2001: Brazil legislature passes sweeping changes to the Civil Code granting equal rights to women in marriage and divorce, in household decision-making authority, and in a wide range of family matters.

Senegal 1999 Senegalese women win national ban on female circumcision.

Germany 2001: Women gain right to enter all divisions of the German military; previously, women were only allowed to serve the military in medical staff positions and musical units.

Austria 1997 The Vienna Philharmonic agrees to admit women as players; it had been an all-male institution since its founding in 1842.

Chad 2002: Parliament passes a law guaranteeing protection for reproductive health rights. The new law makes it an offence to engage in any form of sexual violence, including female genital cutting, forced marriage, domestic violence or sexual slavery. Chadians living with HIV/AIDS are also guaranteed basic health care and confidentiality, according to the provisions of the law. It also codifies the right of Chadians to decide freely when and whom to marry, and guarantees them the right to information about family planning methods.

Peru 1997: Repeal of 1924 law allowing men who rape women to escape punishment by marrying their victims. The law also allowed men involved in a gang rape to go free if one of the men married the woman.

" It is not acceptable for women to constitute 70 percent of the world's 1.3 billion absolute poor. Nor is it acceptable for women to work two-thirds of the world's working hours, but earn only one-tenth of the world's income and own less than one-tenth of the world's property. Many fundamental changes must be made. "

Noleen Heyzer
UNIFEM Director
Plenary Address to the Fourth World
Conference on Women, 1995

Lithuania 2002: The government repeals a requirement that women undergo a gynecological exam to qualify for a driver's license. The law was based on a medical assumption that certain "women's diseases" could cause sufficient pain to inhibit driving.

> Never doubt that a small group of thoughtful committed citizens can change the world; indeed, it's the only thing that ever has.
>
> Margaret Mead
> 1901–78

Turkey 2001: Turkish parliament adopts a revision to the country's Civil Code formally recognizing women's equality. Under the revised code, women no longer need their husband's permission to work outside the home. Married women will now enjoy property rights and will be able to keep their maiden names if they choose. Women will also be able to sue for divorce if their husbands commit adultery and will be entitled to alimony and compensation. The Flying Broom, a Turkish women's rights group, hailed the new code as an "historic turning point."

Jordan 2002
New marital law allows women to initiate divorces.

China 1996: First battered women's shelter opens.

Palestinian Territories 1995: Birzeit University establishes the first Women's Studies program at a Palestinian university.

Afghanistan 2002: First women's reproductive health center opens in Kabul.

Iran 2002: Parliament approves a bill granting women the right to seek a divorce in court – a right women have not had since the 1979 Islamic Revolution. The Guardian Council is likely to block passage of the bill into law, but parliamentary approval sets an important precedent.

Thailand 2007: Parliament passes a law that criminalizes marital rape.

Botswana 1998 First woman appointed to serve as a High Court Justice.

UAE 2008: UAE amends laws to allow women to become judges.

Vietnam 2002: Government bans polygamy and dowries in marriage.

Bahrain 2002: Women allowed to vote and run for all elected offices.

Malaysia 2000: Women lawyers allowed to wear trousers in court.

Somalia 1992: Save Somali Women and Children (SSWC) founded, uniting women across the five main clans. They formed a Sixth Clan and sent 100 delegates to the Somali National Peace Conference in 2000. The resultant Transitional National Government was 10% female, forcing male clan leaders to recognise war impacts on women and children.

Nepal 2008: first all-women Tibetan protest against Chinese rule held in the streets of Kathmandu.
2002: Reversing 150 years of legal discrimination against women, Nepal's Parliament passed an amendment to the Civil Code that partially legalizes abortion and that institutes sweeping changes in many other discriminatory laws, including inheritance rights, marriage and divorce laws, and laws against sexual violence.

Rwanda 2000: New law gives women the right to inherit property on equal terms with men.

South Africa 1994: New constitution grants equal rights between men and women, and equal rights for gays and lesbians.

Australia 2002: The Australian Capital Territory becomes the first state or territory in Australia to completely remove abortion from the criminal code.

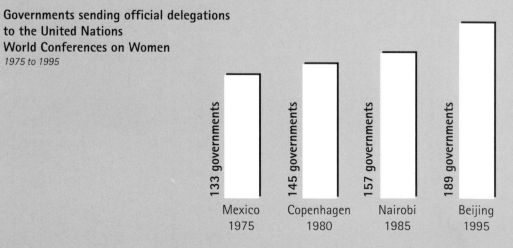

**Governments sending official delegations
to the United Nations
World Conferences on Women**
1975 to 1995

133 governments

Mexico
1975

145 governments

Copenhagen
1980

157 governments

Nairobi
1985

189 governments

Beijing
1995

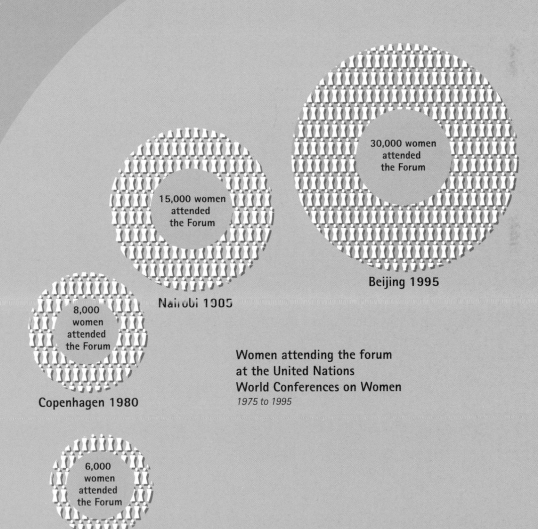

30,000 women
attended
the Forum

Beijing 1995

15,000 women
attended
the Forum

Nairobi 1985

8,000
women
attended
the Forum

Copenhagen 1980

6,000
women
attended
the Forum

Mexico 1975

**Women attending the forum
at the United Nations
World Conferences on Women**
1975 to 1995

Demography and Health

	1 Population 2006		2 Households Average number of people per household 2006	3 Marriage Average age at marriage various dates 1990–2002	4 Motherhood Average number of childbirths per woman 2000 or latest available data
	thousands	% of women			
Afghanistan	–	–	–	–	–
Albania	3,172	50%	4.2	22.9	2.2
Algeria	33,351	49%	4.9	25.9	2.5
Angola	16,557	51%		–	6.8
Argentina	39,134	51%	3.6	23.3	2.4
Armenia	3,010	53%	4.1	23.0	1.3
Australia	20,701	50%	3.8	28.7	1.8
Austria	8,281	51%	2.6	26.1	1.4
Azerbaijan	8,484	51%	4.7	23.9	1.7
Bahamas	327	51%	3.8	27.2	2.1
Bahrain	739	43%	5.9	25.6	2.5
Bangladesh	155,991	49%	4.8	18.7	3.2
Barbados	293	51%	3.5	31.8	1.5
Belarus	9,733	53%	–	22.8	1.2
Belgium	10,541	50%	2.6	27.9	1.6
Belize	298	49%	4.6	26.2	3.4
Benin	8,760	50%	5.9	19.9	5.9
Bhutan	649	47%	–	20.5	2.9
Bolivia	9,354	50%	4.2	22.8	4.0
Bosnia and Herzegovina	3,926	51%	–	–	1.3
Botswana	1,858	50%	4.2	26.9	3.2
Brazil	189,323	50%	3.8	23.4	2.3
Brunei	382	48%		25.1	2.5
Bulgaria	7,693	51%	2.7	21.1	1.3
Burkina Faso	14,359	50%	6.2	18.9	6.4
Burma	48,379	50%		24.5	2.2
Burundi	8,173	51%	4.7	22.5	6.8
Cambodia	14,197	51%	5.2	22.5	3.6
Cameroon	18,175	50%	5.2	20.2	4.9
Canada	32,649	50%	2.6	26.8	1.5
Cape Verde	519	52%	–	–	–
Central African Republic	4,265	51%	5.2	19.7	5.0
Chad	10,468	50%	5.1	18.1	6.5
Chile	16,433	50%	3.4	23.4	2.0
China	1,319,132	48%	3.4	23.3	1.7
Colombia	45,558	51%	4.8	23.1	2.5
Comoros	614	50%	–	–	4.9
Congo	3,689	50%	10.5	–	4.8
Congo, Dem. Rep.	60,644	50%	5.4	–	6.7
Costa Rica	4,399	49%	4.0	20.9	2.3
Côte d'Ivoire	18,914	49%	5.4	22.0	5.1
Croatia	4,441	52%	3.0	26.2	1.3
Cuba	11,267	49%	4.2	–	1.6
Cyprus	771	51%	3.3	23.1	1.6

5 Maternal Mortality Deaths of mothers per 100,000 live births 2000	6 Contraception % of married women using "modern" contraception 2001 or latest available data	7 HIV / AIDS 2005			
		Number living with HIV / AIDS	% living with HIV/AIDS	AIDS deaths in 2001	
1,900	4%	<1,000	<0.1%	<100	Afghanistan
55	8%	–	–	<100	Albania
140	50%	19,000	0.1%	9,800	Algeria
1,700	5%	320,000	3.7%	30,000	Angola
82	0%	130,000	0.6%	4,300	Argentina
55	22%	2,900	0.1%	<500	Armenia
8	72%	16,000	0.1%	<500	Australia
4	47%	12,000	0.3%	<100	Austria
94	12%	5,400	0.1%	<100	Azerbaijan
60	–	6,800	3.3%	5,800	Bahamas
28	–	<1,000	–	–	Bahrain
380	47%	11,000	<0.1%	<500	Bangladesh
95	–	2,700	1.5%	2,700	Barbados
35	42%	20,000	0.3%	–	Belarus
10	74%	14,000	0.3%	<100	Belgium
140	–	3,700	2.5%	<500	Belize
850	7%	87,000	1.8%	9,600	Benin
420	19%	<500	<0.1%	<100	Bhutan
420	35%	7,000	0.1%	<500	Bolivia
31	16%	<500	<0.1%	–	Bosnia and Herzegovina
100	39%	270,000	24.1%	18,000	Botswana
260	70%	620,000	0.5%	14,000	Brazil
37	–	<100	<0.1%	<100	Brunei
32	26%	<500	<0.1%	–	Bulgaria
1,000	9%	270,000	2.0%	12,000	Burkina Faso
360	33%	360,000	1.3%	37,000	Burma
1,000	10%	150,000	3.3%	13,000	Burundi
450	19%	130,000	1.6%	16,000	Cambodia
730	13%	510,000	5.4%	46,000	Cameroon
6	73%	–	0.3%	56,000	Canada
150	–	–	–	–	Cape Verde
1,100	7%	250,000	10.7%	24,000	Central African Republic
1,100	1%	180,000	3.5%	11,000	Chad
31	0%	28,000	0.3%	<500	Chile
56	83%	650,000	0.1%	31,000	China
130	64%	160,000	0.6%	8,200	Colombia
480	–	<500	<0.1%	<100	Comoros
510	–	120,000	5.3%	11,000	Congo
990	4%	1,000,000	3.2%	90,000	Congo, Dem. Rep.
43	71%	7,400	0.3%	<100	Costa Rica
690	7%	750,000	7.1%	65,000	Côte d'Ivoire
8	0%	<500	<0.1%	–	Croatia
33	72%	4,800	0.1%	4,300	Cuba
47	–	<500	–	–	Cyprus

Demography and Health

	1 Population 2006		2 Households Average number of people per household 2006	3 Marriage Average age at marriage various dates 1990–2002	4 Motherhood Average number of childbirths per woman 2000 or latest available data
	thousands	% of women			
Czech Republic	10,270	51%	2.4	25.3	1.2
Denmark	5,437	50%	2.2	30.7	1.8
Djibouti	819	50%	–	–	4.5
Dominican Republic	9,615	50%	3.9	21.3	3.0
Ecuador	13,202	50%	3.5	21.5	2.8
Egypt	74,166	50%	4.7	22.3	3.2
El Salvador	6,762	51%	–	22.3	2.9
Equatorial Guinea	496	50%	7.5	–	5.6
Eritrea	4,692	51%	–	19.6	5.5
Estonia	1,342	54%	2.4	22.1	1.4
Ethiopia	77,154	50%	4.8	20.5	5.8
Fiji	833	49%	5.4	22.9	3.0
Finland	5,266	51%	2.2	30.2	1.8
France	61,257	51%	2.5	30.2	1.9
Gabon	1,311	50%	5.2	22.1	3.4
Gambia	1,663	50%	8.9	19.6	5.2
Georgia	4,433	53%	3.5	24.3	1.5
Germany	82,375	51%	2.3	–	1.3
Ghana	23,008	49%	5.1	21.2	4.4
Greece	11,147	50%	2.8	24.5	1.3
Guatemala	13,029	51%	4.4	20.5	4.6
Guinea	9,181	49%	–	18.7	5.8
Guinea-Bissau	1,646	51%	–	–	7.1
Guyana	739	49%	–	27.8	2.4
Haiti	9,446	50%	4.2	22.3	4.0
Honduras	6,969	50%	4.4	20.4	3.7
Hungary	10,067	52%	2.7	26.3	1.3
Iceland	302	49%	–	30.5	2.0
India	1,109,811	48%	5.3	19.9	3.1
Indonesia	223,042	50%	4.0	22.5	2.4
Iran	70,098	49%	4.8	22.1	2.1
Iraq	–	–	7.7	22.3	–
Ireland	4,268	50%	3.1	30.9	2.0
Israel	7,049	50%	3.5	25.0	2.9
Italy	58,843	51%	2.8	28.4	1.3
Jamaica	2,667	50%	3.5	33.2	2.6
Japan	127,756	51%	2.7	28.6	1.3
Jordan	5,538	48%	6.2	24.0	3.5
Kazakhstan	15,308	52%	–	23.4	2.0
Kenya	36,553	50%	4.6	21.7	5.0
Korea, North	23,708	51%	3.8	–	1.2
Korea, South	48,418	50%	4.4	26.1	–
Kuwait	2,599	40%	6.4	25.2	2.3
Kyrgyzstan	5,192	51%	4.4	21.9	2.5

5 Maternal Mortality Deaths of mothers per 100,000 live births 2000	6 Contraception % of married women using "modern" contraception 2001 or latest available data	7 HIV / AIDS 2005			
		Number living with HIV / AIDS	% living with HIV/AIDS	AIDS deaths in 2001	
9	63%	1,500	0.1%	<100	Czech Republic
5	72%	5,600	0.2%	<100	Denmark
730	–	15,000	3.1%	1,200	Djibouti
150	66%	66,000	1.1%	66,000	Dominican Republic
130	50%	23,000	0.3%	1,600	Ecuador
84	57%	5,300	<0.1%	4,300	Egypt
150	61%	36,000	0.9%	2,500	El Salvador
880	–	8,900	3.2%	<1000	Equatorial Guinea
630	5%	59,000	2.4%	5,600	Eritrea
63	56%	10,000	1.3%	–	Estonia
850	6%	–	–	–	Ethiopia
75	–	<1,000	0.1%	<100	Fiji
6	75%	1,900	0.1%	<100	Finland
17	69%	130,000	0.4%	1,500	France
420	12%	60,000	7.9%	4,700	Gabon
540	9%	20,000	2.4%	1,300	Gambia
32	27%	5,600	0.2%	<500	Georgia
8	72%	49,000	0.1%	<1,000	Germany
540	19%	320,000	2.3%	29,000	Ghana
9	0%	9,300	0.2%	<100	Greece
240	34%	61,000	0.9%	2,700	Guatemala
740	4%	85,000	1.5%	7,100	Guinea
1,100	4%	32,000	3.8%	2,700	Guinea-Bissau
170	–	12,000	2.4%	1,200	Guyana
680	22%	190,000	3.8%	180,000	Haiti
110	51%	63,000	1.5%	3,700	Honduras
16	68%	3,200	0.1%	–	Hungary
0	–	<500	0.2%	<100	Iceland
540	43%	5,700,000	0.9%	–	India
230	57%	170,000	0.1%	5,500	Indonesia
76	56%	66,000	–	1,600	Iran
250	10%	–	–	–	Iraq
5	–	5,000	0.2%	<100	Ireland
17	52%	4,000	–	–	Israel
5	39%	150,000	0.5%	3,000	Italy
87	63%	25,000	1.5%	24,000	Jamaica
10	51%	...17,000	<0.1%	14,000	Japan
41	41%	<1,000	0.0%	–.	Jordan
210	53%	12,000	0.1%	<1,000	Kazakhstan
1,000	32%	1,300,000	6.1%	40,000	Kenya
67	53%	–	–	–	Korea, North
20	67%	13,000	<0.1%	<500	Korea, South
5	41%	<1,000	–	–	Kuwait
110	49%	4,000	0.1%	<1,000	Kyrgyzstan

111

Demography and Health

	1 Population 2006		2 Households Average number of people per household 2006	3 Marriage Average age at marriage various dates 1990–2002	4 Motherhood Average number of childbirths per woman 2000 or latest available data
	thousands	% of women			
Laos	5,759	50%	6.1	20.8	3.6
Latvia	2,288	54%	3.0	26.9	1.2
Lebanon	4,055	51%	–	–	2.3
Lesotho	1,995	53%	5.0	21.3	3.8
Liberia	3,579	50%	4.8	20.2	3.0
Libya	6,039	48%	–	29.2	–
Lithuania	3,395	53%	2.6	24.8	1.3
Luxembourg	462	50%	2.6	26.0	1.7
Macedonia	2,036	50%	3.6	22.9	1.6
Madagascar	19,159	50%	4.9	20.6	5.3
Malawi	13,571	50%	4.4	18.9	6.0
Malaysia	26,114	49%	4.5	25.1	2.9
Maldives	300	49%	6.6	21.8	2.8
Mali	11,968	51%	5.6	18.4	6.7
Malta	406	50%	–		1.5
Mauritania	3,044	49%	–	22.1	4.8
Mauritius	1,253	50%	3.9	23.8	1.9
Mexico	104,221	51%	4.4	22.7	2.4
Moldova	3,833	52%	–	21.1	1.5
Mongolia	2,585	50%	4.4	23.7	2.1
Montenegro*	601	51%	–	–	
Morocco	30,497	51%	5.9	25.3	2.5
Mozambique	20,971	51%	4.4	18.0	5.5
Namibia	2,047	51%	5.3	26.4	3.6
Nepal	27,641	50%	5.4	19.0	3.7
Netherlands	16,340	50%	2.3	29.9	1.7
New Zealand	4,185	50%	2.8	25.4	2.0
Nicaragua	5,532	50%	5.3	20.6	3.0
Niger	13,737	49%	6.4	17.6	7.4
Nigeria	144,720	50%	5.0	21.4	5.8
Norway	4,660	50%	2.7	31.4	1.8
Oman	2,546	44%	7.1	21.7	3.7
Pakistan	159,002	48%	6.8	21.3	4.0
Palestine Authority	3,775	49%	7.1	21.7	5.6
Panama	3,288	49%	4.1	21.9	2.7
Papua New Guinea	6,202	49%	4.5	20.8	4.3
Paraguay	6,016	49%	4.6	21.5	3.5
Peru	27,589	50%	–	23.1	2.7
Philippines	86,264	50%	5.3	24.1	3.5
Poland	38,129	51%	3.2	25.2	1.3
Portugal	10,589	51%	2.8	23.9	1.5
Qatar	821	33%	–	26.3	2.9
Romania	21,590	51%	2.7	24.1	1.3

* Data for Serbia and Montenegro pre-date their separation in 2006 and apply to the country as a single entity.

5 Maternal Mortality Deaths of mothers per 100,000 live births 2000	6 Contraception % of married women using "modern" contraception 2001 or latest available data	7 HIV / AIDS 2005			
		Number living with HIV / AIDS	% living with HIV/AIDS	AIDS deaths in 2001	
650	29%	3,700	0.2%	<100	Laos
42	39%	10,000	0.8%	<500	Latvia
150	37%	2,900	0.1%	1,600	Lebanon
550	35%	270,000	23.2%	23,000	Lesotho
760	6%	–	–	–	Liberia
97	26%	–	–	–	Libya
13	31%	3,300	0.2%	<1,000	Lithuania
28	–	<1,000	0.2%	<100	Luxembourg
23	0%	<500	<0.1%	<100	Macedonia
550	18%	49,000	0.5%	2,900	Madagascar
1,800	26%	940,000	14.1%	78,000	Malawi
41	30%	69,000	0.5%	400	Malaysia
110	–	–	0.5%	–	Maldives
1,200	6%	130,000	1.7%	11,000	Mali
–	–	–	0.1%	<100	Malta
1,000	5%	12,000	0.7%	<1000	Mauritania
24	41%	4,100	0.6%	<100	Mauritius
83	60%	180,000	0.3%	6,200	Mexico
36	43%	29,000	1.1%	1,400	Moldova
110	54%	–	<0.1%	<100	Mongolia
–	33%	38,163	0.2%	<100	Montenegro*
220	55%	19,000	0.1%	17,000	Morocco
1,000	12%	1,800,000	16.1%	140,000	Mozambique
300	43%	230,000	19.6%	17,000	Namibia
740	35%	75,000	0.5%	5,100	Nepal
16	76%	18,000	0.2%	<100	Netherlands
7	72%	1,400	0.1%	–	New Zealand
230	66%	7,300	0.2%	<500	Nicaragua
1,600	4%	79,000	1.1%	7,600	Niger
800	8%	2,900,000	3.9%	220,000	Nigeria
16	69%	2,500	0.1%	<100	Norway
87	18%	–	–	–	Oman
500	20%	85,000	0.1%	3,000	Pakistan
100	37%	–	–	–	Palestine Authority
160	0%	17,000	0.9%	<1,000	Panama
300	20%	80,000	1.8%	3,300	Papua New Guinea
170	61%	13,000	0.4%	<500	Paraguay
410	47%	93,000	0.6%	5,600	Peru
200	33%	12,000	<0.1%	<1,000	Philippines
13	19%	25,000	0.1%	<1,000	Poland
5	0%	32,000	0.4%	<1,000	Portugal
140	–	–	–	–	Qatar
49	30%	7,000	<0.1%	–	Romania

Demography and Health

	1 Population 2006		2 Households Average number of people per household 2006	3 Marriage Average age at marriage various dates 1990–2002	4 Motherhood Average number of childbirths per woman 2000 or latest available data
	thousands	% of women			
Russia	142,500	53%	2.8	21.8	1.3
Rwanda	9,464	52%	4.7	22.7	6.0
Samoa	185	48%	7.3	23.9	4.4
Saudi Arabia	23,679	45%	6.1	21.7	3.8
Senegal	12,072	50%	–	21.5	5.2
Serbia*	7,439	50%	2.9	23.1	–
Seychelles	85	–	4.2	–	–
Sierra Leone	5,743	51%	6.8	19.8	6.5
Singapore	4,484	49%	4.4	26.5	1.4
Slovakia	5,390	51%	2.9	25.4	1.2
Slovenia	2,007	51%	3.1	29.8	1.2
Solomon Islands	484	48%	6.3	–	4.4
Somalia	8,445	50%	–	–	–
South Africa	47,391	51%	4.0	27.9	2.8
Spain	44,121	50%	3.3	26.0	1.3
Sri Lanka	19,886	50%	3.8	25.3	2.0
Sudan	37,707	50%	5.8	22.7	4.8
Suriname	455	50%	–	–	2.6
Swaziland	1,138	52%	5.4	26.0	3.9
Sweden	9,084	50%	2.2	32.3	1.7
Switzerland	7,491	51%	2.4	29.1	1.4
Syria	19,408	49%	6.3	–	3.5
Tajikistan	6,640	50%	–	21.2	3.8
Tanzania	39,459	50%	4.9	20.5	5.7
Thailand	63,444	51%	3.8	23.5	1.8
Togo	6,410	50%	–	21.3	5.4
Trinidad and Tobago	1,328	51%	3.7	26.8	1.6
Tunisia	10,128	49%	8.0	26.6	2.0
Turkey	72,975	50%	5.0	22.0	2.2
Turkmenistan	4,899	51%	–	23.4	2.8
Uganda	29,899	50%	4.9	19.6	6.7
Ukraine	46,788	54%	–	21.7	1.2
United Arab Emirates	4,248	32%	–	23.1	2.5
United Kingdom	60,550	50%	2.3	26.4	1.7
United States	299,398	50%	2.7	26.3	2.0
Uruguay	3,314	51%	3.3	23.3	2.2
Uzbekistan	26,540	50%	–	20.6	2.7
Venezuela	27,021	50%	4.4	22.1	2.7
Vietnam	84,108	50%	4.6	22.1	2.3
Yemen	21,732	49%	6.7	20.7	6.0
Zambia	11,696	50%	5.3	20.6	5.6
Zimbabwe	13,228	50%	4.8	21.1	3.6

Sources: WDI online database **(Col 1)**; Eurostat, World Bank, *World Development Indicators 2006* **(Col 2)**; UN Population Division, *World Fertility Report 2003* **(Col 3)**; UN, *Human Development Report 2007/2008* **(Col 4)**

* Data for Serbia and Montenegro pre-date their separation in 2006 and apply to the country as a single entity.

5 **Maternal Mortality** Deaths of mothers per 100,000 live births *2000*	6 **Contraception** % of married women using "modern" contraception *2001 or latest available data*	7 **HIV / AIDS** *2005*			
		Number living with HIV / AIDS	% living with HIV/AIDS	AIDS deaths in 2001	
67	47%	940,000	1.1%	–	Russia
1,400	4%	190,000	3.1%	21,000	Rwanda
130	–	–	–	–	Samoa
23	29%	–	–	–	Saudi Arabia
690	8%	61,000	0.9%	5,200	Senegal
–	33%	10,000	0.2%	<100	Serbia*
–	–	–	–	–	Seychelles
2,000	4%	48,000	1.6%	4,600	Sierra Leone
30	53%	5,500	0.3%	<100	Singapore
3	41%	<500	<0.1%	–	Slovakia
17	59%	<500	<0.1%	<100	Slovenia
–	–	–	–	–	Solomon Islands
1,100	0%	44,000	0.9%	4,100	Somalia
230	55%	5,500,000	18.8%	320,000	South Africa
4	67%	140,000	0.6%	2,000	Spain
92	50%	5,000	<0.1%	<500	Sri Lanka
590	7%	350,000	1.6%	330,000	Sudan
110	26%	5,200	1.9%	<500	Suriname
370	–	220,000	33.4%	16,000	Swaziland
2	0%	8,000	0.2%	<100	Sweden
7	78%	17,000	0.4%	<100	Switzerland
160	28%	–	–	–	Syria
100	27%	4,900	0.1%	<100	Tajikistan
1,500	20%	1,400,000	8.5%	140,000	Tanzania
44	70%	580,000	1.5%	21,000	Thailand
570	9%	110,000	3.2%	9,100	Togo
160	33%	27,000	2.6%	25,000	Trinidad and Tobago
120	53%	8,700	0.1%	4,400	Tunisia
70	38%	<2,000	–	–	Turkey
31	53%	<500	<0.1%		Turkmenistan
880	18%	1,000,000	6.7%	91,000	Uganda
35	38%	410,000	1.4%	22,000	Ukraine
54	24%	–	–	–	United Arab Emirates
13	81%	88,000	0.2%	<1000	United Kingdom
17	68%	1,200,000	0.6%	1,100,000	United States
27	0%	9,600	0.5%	<500	Uruguay
24	63%	31,000	0.2%	<500	Uzbekistan
96	0%	110,000	0.7%	6,100	Venezuela
130	57%	260,000	0.5%	13,000	Vietnam
570	10%	–	–	–	Yemen
750	23%	1,100,000	17.0%	98,000	Zambia
1,100	50%	1,700,000	20.1%	180,000	Zimbabwe

UNICEF, *State of World's Children 2007* **(Col 5)**; UNFPA, *State of the World's Population 2007* **(Col 6)**; UNAIDS/WHO, *Report on the Global AIDS epidemic 2006* **(Col 7)**

School, Work, Power

	1 Gender Development Index Country rank 2007	2 The Vote Date of women's suffrage on equal terms with men	3 Women Working % of women work for pay 2005	4 Workplaces 1995–2005 % of economically active women working in:		
				agriculture	industry	services
Afghanistan	–	1965	–	–	–	–
Albania	60	1945	49%	–	–	49%
Algeria	94	1962	36%	22%	28%	–
Angola	141	1975	74%	–	–	87%
Argentina	36	1947	53%	1%	11%	88%
Armenia	74	1921	48%	–	–	–
Australia	2	1902	56%	3%	9%	88%
Austria	19	1918	49%	6%	13%	81%
Azerbaijan	86	1921	60%	37%	9%	54%
Bahamas	48	1962	64%	–	5%	94%
Bahrain	42	2001	29%	–	–	–
Bangladesh	120	1956	53%	59%	18%	23%
Barbados	30	1919	65%	3%	8%	78%
Belarus	56	1948	53%	–	–	–
Belgium	14	1954	44%	1%	11%	82%
Belize	–	–	43%	6%	12%	83%
Benin	144	1956	54%	–	–	–
Bhutan	–	1953	47%	–	–	–
Bolivia	102	1952	63%	3%	14%	82%
Bosnia and Herzegovina	–	1949	58%	–	–	–
Botswana	108	1965	45%	19%	13%	58%
Brazil	59	1932	57%	16%	13%	71%
Brunei	31	no one votes	44%	–	11%	88%
Bulgaria	50	1944	41%	7%	29%	64%
Burkina Faso	153	1956	78%	–	–	–
Burma	–	1935	68%	0%	0%	0%
Burundi	146	1961	92%	–	–	–
Cambodia	113	1956	74%	75%	10%	15%
Cameroon	125	1956	52%	68%	4%	23%
Canada	4	1918	61%	2%	11%	88%
Cape Verde	92	–	34%	–	–	–
Central African Republic	152	1956	70%	–	–	–
Chad	151	1956	66%	–	–	–
Chile	40	1948	37%	6%	12%	83%
China	72	1949	69%	–	–	–
Colombia	65	1954	61%	8%	16%	76%
Comoros	115	1956	58%	–	–	–
Congo	119	1956	56%	–	–	–
Congo, Dem. Rep.	147	1967	61%	–	–	–
Costa Rica	47	1949	45%	5%	13%	82%
Côte d'Ivoire	145	1952	39%	–	–	–
Croatia	46	1945	45%	19%	18%	63%
Cuba	49	1934	44%	10%	14%	76%
Cyprus	27	1960	54%	4%	11%	85%

5 School % enrolled in primary school 2005		6 University Women as a % of students 2005	7 Literacy 2005		8 Government Women as % of members of lower or single House 2008	
girls	boys		% of women who are illiterate	% of men who are illiterate		
64%	108%	–	87%	57%	28%	Afghanistan
105%	106%	62%	2%	1%	7%	Albania
107%	116%	57%	40%	20%	8%	Algeria
–	–	40%	40%	17%	15%	Angola
0%	113%	55%	3%	3%	40%	Argentina
96%	92%	56%	1%	1%	9%	Armenia
104%	104%	55%	1%	1%	27%	Australia
106%	106%	53%	1%	1%	33%	Austria
95%	97%	47%	2%	1%	11%	Azerbaijan
101%	101%	–	5%	5%	12%	Bahamas
104%	105%	69%	16%	11%	3%	Bahrain
111%	107%	35%	59%	46%	–	Bangladesh
108%	108%	–	–	0%	–	Barbados
100%	103%	58%	1%	1%	29%	Belarus
103%	104%	51%	1%	1%	35%	Belgium
125%	130%	70%	–	–	0%	Belize
85%	107%	–	77%	52%	11%	Benin
–	–	–	–	–	9%	Bhutan
113%	113%	–	19%	7%	17%	Bolivia
–	–	–	6%	1%	12%	Bosnia and Herzegovina
105%	107%	52%	18%	20%	11%	Botswana
135%	146%	57%	11%	12%	9%	Brazil
107%	108%	69%	10%	5%	–	Brunei
104%	106%	52%	2%	1%	22%	Bulgaria
51%	64%	–	83%	69%	15%	Burkina Faso
101%	99%	–	14%	6%	–	Burma
78%	91%	25%	48%	33%	31%	Burundi
129%	139%	32%	36%	15%	20%	Cambodia
107%	126%	–	40%	23%	14%	Cameroon
99%	100%	58%	1%	1%	21%	Canada
105%	111%	51%	24%	12%	18%	Cape Verde
44%	67%	–	66%	35%	11%	Central African Republic
62%	92%	–	87%	59%	5%	Chad
101%	106%	52%	4%	4%	15%	Chile
112%	113%	47%	13%	5%	21%	China
111%	113%	57%	7%	7%	8%	Colombia
80%	91%	39%	36%	36%	3%	Comoros
84%	91%	16%	21%	9%	7%	Congo
54%	69%	–	46%	19%	8%	Congo, Dem. Rep.
109%	110%	–	5%	5%	37%	Costa Rica
63%	80%	–	61%	39%	9%	Côte d'Ivoire
94%	95%	55%	3%	1%	21%	Croatia
99%	104%	62%	1%	1%	43%	Cuba
101%	101%	76%	5%	1%	14%	Cyprus

School, Work, Power

	1 Gender Development Index Country rank 2007	2 The Vote Date of women's suffrage on equal terms with men	3 Women Working % of women work for pay 2005	4 Workplaces 1995–2005 % of economically active women working in:		
				agriculture	industry	services
Czech Republic	29	1920	55%	3%	27%	71%
Denmark	11	1915	59%	2%	12%	86%
Djibouti	128	1957	53%	–	1%	88%
Dominican Republic	73	1942	46%	2%	15%	83%
Ecuador	–	1929	60%	4%	12%	84%
Egypt	–	1956	20%	39%	6%	55%
El Salvador	91	1950	47%	3%	22%	75%
Equatorial Guinea	110	1963	50%	–	–	–
Eritrea	136	1955	58%	–	–	–
Estonia	41	1918	52%	4%	24%	72%
Ethiopia	148	1955	71%	91%	3%	6%
Fiji	81	1963	52%	–	–	–
Finland	8	1906	57%	3%	12%	84%
France	7	1944	48%	3%	12%	84%
Gabon	104	1956	61%	–	–	–
Gambia	132	1960	59%	–	–	–
Georgia	–	1921	50%	57%	4%	38%
Germany	20	1918	51%	2%	16%	82%
Ghana	116	1954	70%	50%	15%	36%
Greece	24	1952	44%	14%	10%	76%
Guatemala	103	1946	34%	18%	23%	56%
Guinea	140	1958	79%	–	–	–
Guinea-Bissau	155	1977	61%	–	–	–
Guyana	87	1966	44%	16%	20%	61%
Haiti	–	1950	56%	37%	6%	57%
Honduras	100	1955	54%	13%	23%	63%
Hungary	34	1945	42%	3%	21%	76%
Iceland	1	1915	71%	4%	11%	85%
India	112	1950	34%	–	–	–
Indonesia	93	1945	51%	45%	15%	40%
Iran	83	1963	39%	34%	28%	37%
Iraq	–	1980	–	–	–	–
Ireland	15	1922	53%	1%	12%	86%
Israel	21	1948	50%	1%	11%	88%
Italy	17	1945	37%	3%	18%	79%
Jamaica	89	1944	54%	9%	5%	86%
Japan	13	1945	48%	5%	18%	77%
Jordan	79	1974	28%	2%	13%	83%
Kazakhstan	64	1924	65%	32%	10%	58%
Kenya	126	1963	69%	16%	10%	75%
Korea, North	...	1946	0%	0%	0%	0%
Korea, South	26	1948	50%	9%	17%	74%
Kuwait	32	2005	49%	–	–	–
Kyrgyzstan	101	1918	55%	55%	7%	38%

5 School % enrolled in primary school 2005		6 University Women as a % of students 2005	7 Literacy 2005		8 Government Women as % of members of lower or single House 2008	
girls	boys		% of women who are illiterate	% of men who are illiterate		
100%	102%	52%	1%	1%	16%	Czech Republic
99%	98%	59%	1%	1%	38%	Denmark
36%	44%	39%	20%	20%	14%	Djibouti
110%	115%	65%	13%	13%	20%	Dominican Republic
117%	117%	–	10%	8%	25%	Ecuador
97%	104%	–	40%	17%	2%	Egypt
111%	115%	55%	21%	18%	17%	El Salvador
111%	117%	–	19%	7%	18%	Equatorial Guinea
57%	71%	12%	28%	28%	22%	Eritrea
99%	102%	62%	1%	1%	21%	Estonia
94%	107%	25%	77%	50%	22%	Ethiopia
105%	107%	52%	4%	4%	–	Fiji
99%	100%	54%	1%	1%	42%	Finland
110%	111%	55%	1%	1%	18%	France
129%	130%	–	20%	11%	17%	Gabon
84%	79%	19%	50%	50%	9%	Gambia
94%	93%	50%	–	–	9%	Georgia
101%	101%	48%	1%	1%	32%	Germany
93%	94%	34%	50%	34%	11%	Ghana
101%	101%	53%	6%	2%	15%	Greece
109%	118%	42%	37%	25%	12%	Guatemala
74%	88%	–	82%	57%	19%	Guinea
–	–	–	40%	40%	14%	Guinea-Bissau
131%	133%	65%	1%	1%	29%	Guyana
–	–	–	43%	43%	4%	Haiti
113%	113%	58%	20%	20%	23%	Honduras
97%	99%	58%	1%	1%	11%	Hungary
98%	101%	65%	1%	1%	33%	Iceland
116%	123%	39%	52%	27%	9%	India
115%	119%	42%	13%	6%	12%	Indonesia
122%	100%	55%	23%	12%	3%	Iran
89%	108%	39%	36%	16%	26%	Iraq
106%	108%	58%	1%	1%	13%	Ireland
110%	109%	57%	2%	2%	14%	Israel
102%	103%	57%	2%	1%	–	Italy
94%	95%	73%	14%	26%	13%	Jamaica
100%	100%	41%	1%	1%	9%	Japan
96%	95%	49%	13%	5%	6%	Jordan
108%	110%	58%	1%	1%	16%	Kazakhstan
112%	116%	35%	30%	22%	7%	Kenya
–	–	–	–	–	20%	Korea, North
104%	105%	0%	1%	1%	14%	Korea, South
97%	99%	66%	9%	6%	2%	Kuwait
97%	98%	55%	2%	1%	26%	Kyrgyzstan

School, Work, Power

	1 Gender Development Index Country rank 2007	2 The Vote Date of women's suffrage on equal terms with men	3 Women Working % of women work for pay 2005	4 Workplaces 1995–2005 % of economically active women working in:		
				agriculture	industry	services
Laos	114	1958	54%	89%	3%	8%
Latvia	44	1918	49%	8%	16%	75%
Lebanon	80	1952	32%	–	–	–
Lesotho	118	1965	46%	45%	13%	31%
Liberia	...	1946	–	–	–	–
Libya	61	1963	32%	–	–	–
Lithuania	38	1918	52%	11%	21%	68%
Luxembourg	23	1919	45%	3%	8%	89%
Macedonia	63	1946	41%	19%	30%	51%
Madagascar	121	1959	79%	79%	6%	15%
Malawi	142	1964	85%	–	–	–
Malaysia	57	1957	47%	11%	27%	62%
Maldives	84	1932	49%	5%	24%	39%
Mali	150	1956	73%	–	–	–
Malta	33	–	34%	1%	18%	81%
Mauritania	117	1961	54%	–	–	–
Mauritius	62	1956	43%	9%	29%	62%
Mexico	51	1953	40%	5%	19%	76%
Moldova	96	1917	57%	40%	12%	48%
Mongolia	99	1924	54%	38%	14%	49%
Montenegro*	–	1946	–	–	–	–
Morocco	111	1959	27%	57%	19%	25%
Mozambique	149	1975	85%	–	–	–
Namibia	107	1989	47%	29%	7%	63%
Nepal	127	1951	49%	–	–	–
Netherlands	6	1919	56%	2%	8%	86%
New Zealand	18	1893	60%	5%	11%	84%
Nicaragua	98	1955	36%	10%	17%	52%
Niger	154	1956	71%	–	–	–
Nigeria	138	1978	45%	2%	11%	87%
Norway	3	1913	63%	2%	8%	90%
Oman	66	1996	23%	5%	14%	80%
Pakistan	124	1956	33%	65%	16%	20%
Palestine Authority	–	–	10%	34%	8%	56%
Panama	54	1946	51%	4%	9%	86%
Papua New Guinea	123	1975	72%	–	–	–
Paraguay	85	1961	65%	20%	10%	70%
Peru	75	1979	59%	–	13%	86%
Philippines	76	1937	55%	25%	12%	64%
Poland	35	1918	48%	17%	17%	66%
Portugal	28	1975	56%	13%	21%	66%
Qatar	37	1999	36%	–	3%	97%
Romania	53	1946	50%	33%	25%	42%
Russia	58	1917	54%	8%	21%	71%

* Data for Serbia and Montenegro that pre-date their separation in 2006 apply to the country as a single entity.

5 School % enrolled in primary school 2005		6 University Women as a % of students 2005	7 Literacy 2005		8 Government Women as % of members of lower or single House 2008	
girls	boys		% of women who are illiterate	% of men who are illiterate		
108%	123%	42%	39%	23%	25%	Laos
91%	94%	63%	1%	1%	20%	Latvia
105%	108%	54%	6%	6%	5%	Lebanon
131%	132%	58%	10%	26%	25%	Lesotho
–	–	–	54%	42%	13%	Liberia
105%	106%	52%	25%	7%	8%	Libya
97%	98%	59%	1%	1%	23%	Lithuania
100%	100%	54%	1%	1%	23%	Luxembourg
98%	98%	–	6%	2%	29%	Macedonia
136%	141%	48%	35%	23%	8%	Madagascar
124%	121%	35%	46%	25%	13%	Malawi
96%	96%	58%	15%	8%	11%	Malaysia
93%	95%	–	4%	4%	12%	Maldives
59%	74%	31%	84%	67%	10%	Mali
95%	101%	56%	11%	14%	9%	Malta
94%	93%	25%	57%	40%	22%	Mauritania
102%	102%	51%	19%	12%	17%	Mauritius
108%	110%	51%	10%	7%	23%	Mexico
92%	93%	–	1%	1%	22%	Moldova
119%	117%	62%	2%	2%	7%	Mongolia
–	–	–	6%	1%	11%	Montenegro*
99%	111%	46%	60%	34%	11%	Morocco
96%	114%	33%	75%	45%	35%	Mozambique
100%	99%	55%	16%	13%	27%	Namibia
123%	129%	28%	65%	37%	–	Nepal
106%	108%	51%	1%	1%	39%	Netherlands
102%	102%	59%	1%	1%	33%	New Zealand
110%	113%	52%	23%	23%	19%	Nicaragua
39%	54%	21%	85%	67%	12%	Niger
95%	111%	26%	40%	32%	7%	Nigeria
98%	98%	60%	1%	1%	36%	Norway
82%	81%	54%	16%	13%	0%	Oman
75%	99%	46%	65%	36%	23%	Pakistan
88%	89%	50%	12%	3%	–	Palestine Authority
109%	113%	62%	9%	7%	17%	Panama
70%	80%	–	49%	37%	1%	Papua New Guinea
103%	106%	55%	7%	6%	–	Paraguay
112%	113%	45%	13%	6%	29%	Peru
112%	113%	54%	6%	8%	21%	Philippines
98%	98%	57%	1%	1%	20%	Poland
112%	117%	56%	8%	4%	28%	Portugal
106%	106%	68%	11%	11%	0%	Qatar
106%	108%	55%	4%	2%	9%	Romania
128%	129%	58%	1%	1%	14%	Russia

School, Work, Power

	1 Gender Development Index Country rank 2007	2 The Vote Date of women's suffrage on equal terms with men	3 Women Working % of women work for pay 2005	4 Workplaces 1995–2005 % of economically active women working in:		
				agriculture	industry	services
Rwanda	139	1961	80%	–	–	–
Samoa	71	1990	39%	–	–	–
Saudi Arabia	69	women denied vote	18%	1%	1%	98%
Senegal	134	1956	56%	–	–	–
Serbia*	–	1946	–	–	–	–
Seychelles	–	1948	–	–	–	–
Sierra Leone	156	1961	56%	–	–	–
Singapore	–	1957	51%	–	21%	79%
Slovakia	39	1920	52%	3%	25%	72%
Slovenia	25	1945	54%	9%	25%	65%
Solomon Islands	–	1974	54%	–	–	–
Somalia	–	1958	–	–	–	–
South Africa	106	1994	46%	7%	14%	79%
Spain	12	1931	45%	4%	12%	84%
Sri Lanka	88	1931	35%	40%	35%	25%
Sudan	130	1965	26%	–	–	–
Suriname	77	1953	34%	2%	1%	97%
Swaziland	122	1968	31%	–	–	–
Sweden	5	1919	59%	1%	9%	90%
Switzerland	9	1971	60%	3%	12%	85%
Syria	95	1953	39%	58%	7%	35%
Tajikistan	105	1924	46%	–	–	–
Tanzania	137	1959	86%	84%	1%	15%
Thailand	70	1932	66%	41%	19%	41%
Togo	133	1956	50%	–	–	–
Trinidad and Tobago	55	1946	47%	2%	14%	84%
Tunisia	82	1959	29%	–	–	–
Turkey	78	1930	28%	52%	15%	33%
Turkmenistan	–	1927	61%	–	–	–
Uganda	131	1962	80%	77%	5%	17%
Ukraine	68	1919	49%	17%	21%	62%
United Arab Emirates	43	no one votes	38%	–	14%	86%
United Kingdom	10	1928	55%	1%	9%	90%
United States	16	1920	59%	1%	10%	90%
Uruguay	45	1932	56%	2%	13%	86%
Uzbekistan	97	1938	57%	–	–	–
Venezuela	67	1946	57%	2%	11%	86%
Vietnam	90	1946	72%	60%	14%	26%
Yemen	135	1967	29%	88%	3%	9%
Zambia	143	1964	66%	78%	2%	20%
Zimbabwe	129	1957	64%	–	–	–

Sources: UN, *Human Development Report 2007/08* (**Cols 1, 7**); Inter-Parliamentary Union (**Col 2**); ILO; UN, *Human Development Report 2007/08* (**Cols 3, 4**)

* Data for Serbia and Montenegro pre-date their separation in 2006 apply to the country as a single entity.

5 School % enrolled in primary school 2005		6 University Women as a % of students 2005	7 Literacy 2005		8 Government Women as % of members of lower or single House 2008	
girls	boys		% of women who are illiterate	% of men who are illiterate		
121%	119%	41%	40%	29%	49	Rwanda
100%	100%	–	2%	1%	8%	Samoa
91%	91%	65%	24%	12%	0%	Saudi Arabia
77%	80%	–	71%	49%	22%	Senegal
–	–	–	6%	1%	20%	Serbia*
116%	115%	–	7%	9%	24%	Seychelles
–	–	–	76%	53%	13%	Sierra Leone
–	–	–	11%	3%	25%	Singapore
98%	99%	56%	1%	1%	19%	Slovakia
100%	102%	61%	1%	1%	12%	Slovenia
94%	99%	–	–	–	0%	Solomon Islands
–	–	–	–	–	8%	Somalia
102%	106%	55%	19%	16%	33%	South Africa
105%	108%	54%	1%	1%	36%	Spain
–	–	–	11%	8%	6%	Sri Lanka
56%	65%	–	48%	29%	18%	Sudan
120%	120%	–	13%	8%	26%	Suriname
104%	111%	52%	21%	19%	11%	Swaziland
97%	97%	61%	1%	1%	47%	Sweden
101%	102%	48%	1%	1%	29%	Switzerland
121%	127%	–	26%	12%	12%	Syria
99%	103%	26%	1%	1%	18%	Tajikistan
109%	112%	33%	38%	22%	30%	Tanzania
94%	98%	52%	9%	5%	12%	Thailand
92%	108%	–	61%	31%	11%	Togo
99%	102%	60%	2%	1%	27%	Trinidad and Tobago
108%	111%	–	35%	17%	23%	Tunisia
91%	96%	43%	20%	5%	9%	Turkey
–	–	–	–	1%	16%	Turkmenistan
119%	119%	41%	42%	23%	31%	Uganda
107%	107%	54%	1%	1%	8%	Ukraine
82%	85%	–	12%	11%	23%	United Arab Emirates
107%	107%	55%	1%	1%	20%	United Kingdom
99%	99%	57%	1%	1%	17%	United States
108%	110%	60%	2%	4%	12%	Uruguay
99%	100%	39%	1%	1%	17%	Uzbekistan
104%	106%	–	7%	7%	19%	Venezuela
91%	98%	47%	13%	6%	26%	Vietnam
75%	101%	–	65%	27%	<1%	Yemen
108%	114%	–	40%	24%	15%	Zambia
95%	97%	32%	14%	7%	14%	Zimbabwe

UNESCO, *Global Education Digest 2007* – Number of pupils enrolled in a given level of education, regardless of age, expressed as a percentage of the population in the theoretical age group for the same level of education **(Col 5)**; UNESCO, *Global Education Digest 2007* **(Col 6)**; InterParliamentary Union, www.ipu.org/wmn-e/classif.htm **(Col 7)**

Sources

12–13 Part One WOMEN IN THE WORLD
United Nations Development Programme (UNDP). *Human Development Report*, 2007–08. http://hdr.undp.org/en/

14–15 States Against Discrimination
CEDAW United Nations. Division for the Advancement of Women. www.un.org/womenwatch/daw/cedaw/states.htm

16–17 The State of Women
Taking the measure of women's status Population Reference Bureau (PRB). *2007 World Population Data Sheet*. Washington DC: PRB, 2007; UNDP. *Human Development Report 2007–08*; Richard Hausmann, Laura Tyson, Saadia Zahidi. *The Global Gender Gap Report 2007*. World Economic Forum, 2007

18–19 In Their Place
Restrictions on women US State Department. *Country Reports on Human Rights Practices*, 2007; Human Rights Watch, various reports; news items

20–21 Part Two FAMILIES
Eurostat. *The Social Situation in Europe 2005–06*; UN Economic Commission for Europe. *Trends in Europe & North America 2005*

22–23 Households
The shrinking household Eurostat. *The Social Situation in Europe 2005–06*; World Bank, *World Development Indicators 2006*; UN/ECLAC *Social Panorama of Latin America, 2006*; John Bongaarts. *Household Size and Composition in the Developing World*, Population Council, 2001; Demographic Health Surveys, http://www.measuredhs.com/aboutsurveys/dhs/start.cfm
Women and poverty US Census, American Community Survey
Lone parent households UN Economic Commission for Europe, database. http://w3.unece.org/pxweb/database/stat/Gender.stat.asp
Living alone UN Economic Commission for Europe, http://w3.unece.org/pxweb/database/stat/Gender.stat.asp; Eurostat. *The Social Situation in Europe 2005–06*
Lesbian and gay households in the USA US Bureau of the Census

24–25 Marriage and Divorce
Getting married UN, Population Division. *World Fertility Report, 2003*; United Nations Population Fund (UNFPA). *State of World Population 2005*; United Nations Children's Fund (UNICEF). *A World Fit for Children Statistical Review 2007*; UNICEF. *Early Marriage: A Harmful Traditional Practice*. 2005; Hoda Rashad et al. "Marriage in the Arab World". PRB, 2005
Polygyny in Africa UNICEF. *Early Marriage: A Harmful Traditional Practice*. 2005; Michele Tertilt. "Polygyny, Fertility and Savings" *Journal of Political Economy*, 2005, vol. 113, no. 6]; C. Cook. "Polygyny" *Journal of Black Studies*, 38(2), 2007
Divorce www.divorcemag.com/statistics/statsWorld.shtml

26–27 Lesbian Rights
Lesbians, gays and the law "Behind the Mask" www.mask.org.za/index.php?page=africabycountry; International Lesbian and Gay Association (ILGA). *State-Sponsored Homophobia*, April 2007; Amnesty International. *Sexual Minorities and the Law: A world survey,* July 2006; International Gay & Lesbian Human Rights Commission. *Where Having Sex is a Crime*, 2003
Same-sex partnership recognition Human Rights Campaign, www.hrc.org/about_us/state_laws.asp; ILGA/ Europe, www.ilga-europe.org/europe/issues/marriage_and_partnership/same_sex_marriage_and_partnership_country_by_country; International Gay & Lesbian Human Rights Commission. *Where You Can Marry: Global Summary of Registered Partnership, Domestic Partnership, and Marriage Laws* (November 2003), www.iglhrc.org/site/iglhrc/content.php?type=1&id=91; Amnesty International. *Sexual Minorities and the Law: A world survey*, July 2006; news reports
Global views on homosexuality The PEW Foundation. PEW Forum on Religion & Public Life, 2003. http://pewforum.org/

28–29 Domestic Violence
Violence against women Kishor, S. and K. Johnson. *Profiling Domestic Violence: A Multicountry Study*. Calverton, Maryland: 2004; US Department of State. *Country Reports on Human Rights Practices, 2006*; UNFPA. Violence against Women Fact Sheet. *State of the World Population 2005*, www.unfpa.org/swp/2005/presskit/factsheets/facts_vaw.htm; World Health Organization (WHO). *Multicountry Study on Women's Health & Domestic Violence*, 2006; Amnesty International. *Report 2007, The State of the World's Human Rights*; Human Rights Watch, various reports; Statistics Canada. *Family Violence in Canada: A Statistical profile*, 2005; UK Home Office. *Crime in England & Wales*, 2006/7; WHO. *World Report on Violence and Health*, Geneva: WHO, 2002
Women's justifications of domestic violence Demographic Health Surveys, http://www.measuredhs.com/aboutsurveys/dhs/start.cfm
Suffering in silence WHO. *World Report on Violence and Health*. Geneva: WHO, 2002

30–31 Murder
Murders of women by intimate partners US Department of Justice, Bureau of Justice Statistics. *Sourcebook of Justice Statistics, 2006;* US Department of Justice, Bureau of Justice Statistics. *Criminal Victimization, 2006;* US Department of Justice, Bureau of Justice Statistics. *Homicide Trends in the USA, 2007;* US State Department. *Country Reports on Human Rights Practices, 2006;* Amnesty International. *Report 2007, The State of the World's Human Rights;* UN. Report of the Secretary-General, 2006. In-depth study on all forms of violence against women; United Nations Development Fund for Women (UNIFEM). *Facts & Figures on Violence Against Women*, 2007; Statistics Canada. *Family Violence in Canada: A Statistical profile*, 2005; Human Rights Commission of Pakistan. various reports; Human Rights Watch, 2006; Geneva Centre for the Democratic Control of Armed Forces, 2005. *Women in an Insecure World: Violence Against Women*; Radhila Coomaraswamy. *The Varied Contours of Violence Against Women in South Asia*, 2005; Expert Group Meeting on indicators to measure violence against women. ECLAC, 2007; AlertNet, April 18 2005, "Jordan: special report on honor killings"; news reports
Homicide in the USA US Department of Justice, Bureau of Justice Statistics. *Sourcebook of Justice Statistics, 2001*

32–33 Part Three BIRTHRIGHTS
UNICEF. *State of the World's Children, 2007*

34–35 Motherhood
Births UNDP. *Human Development Report, 2008*
Women want fewer children Demographic & Health Surveys www.measuredhs.com/
Different expectations Demographic & Health Surveys www.measuredhs.com/

36–37 Contraception
Use of contraception UNFPA. *State of the World's Population, 2007*, www.unfpa.org/swp/2007/english/notes/indicators/e_indicator1.pdf; PRB. *Family Planning Worldwide 2002 Data Sheet*, and various reports
Types of contraception PRB. *Family Planning Worldwide 2002 Data Sheet*
Unmet need Gilda Sedgh, Rubina Hussain, Akinrinola Bankole and Susheela Singh. *Women with an Unmet Need for Contraception in Developing Countries and Their Reasons for Not Using a Method*. Occasional Report No. 37 June, 2007, Guttmacher Institute; PRB. *Family Planning Worldwide 2002 Data Sheet*, and various reports
Emergency contraception Office of Population Research, Princeton University, ec.princeton.edu/questions/dedicated.html; International Consortium for Emergency Contraception, www.cecinfo.org/database/pill/viewAllCountry.php
Supplying the world with condoms UNFPA. *Donor Support for Contraceptives and Condoms*, 2002

38–39 Abortion
Legal status of abortion Jones, Rachel et al. Abortion in the United States: Incidence and Access to Services, 2005. *Perspectives on Sexual & Reproductive Health*, Volume 40, Number 1, March 2008; Center for Reproductive Rights, New York, www.reproductiverights.org/pub_fac_abortion_laws.html; "Children by Choice" (Queensland, Australia), www.childrenbychoice.org.au/nwww/auslawprac.htm; National Abortion Federation USA; UN Population Division. *Abortion Policies A Global Review*, 2002–07
Unsafe abortions David A Grimes, Janie Benson, Susheela Singh, Mariana Romero, Bela Ganatra, Friday E Okonofua, Iqbal H Shah. Unsafe abortion: the preventable pandemic. *The Lancet Sexual and Reproductive Health Series*, October 2006; WHO. *Unsafe abortion: global and regional estimates of incidence of unsafe abortion and associated mortality in 2003*. Geneva: WHO, 2007; www.who.int/reproductive-health/publications/unsafeabortion_2003/ua_estimates03.pdf; Sedgh G, Henshaw S, Singh S, Åhman E, Shah IH. Induced abortion: rates and trends worldwide. *Lancet* 2007, 370: 1338–45.
Legal abortion UN Population Division. *World Abortion Policies 2007*, www.un.org/esa/population/publications/2007_Abortion_Policies_Chart/2007AbortionPolicies_wallchart.htm; Sedgh G, Henshaw S, Singh S, Åhman E, Shah IH. Induced abortion: rates and trends worldwide. *Lancet* 2007, 370: 1338–45

40–41 Maternal Mortality
Women who die in pregnancy or childbirth UNICEF. *State of World's Children, 2007*.
Medical causes of maternal mortality WHO. *The World Health Report 2005*. Geneva: WHO, http://www.who.int/; Khan, Khalid, et al, 2006. "WHO analysis of causes of maternal deaths" *The Lancet 367*
Race and mother-death USA Centers for Disease Control. *Safe Motherhood*, 2007; Michael Garenne et al. "Maternal mortality in South Africa in 2001: From census to epidemiology". Presented at UAPS conference, December 2007

42–43 Son Preference
Unnatural selection Census of India 2001 www.censusindia.net/results/provindia2.

html; China StatisticalYearbook 2000; UNDP. *Korea Human Development Report 1998*; US Census Bureau. Son Preference in Asia–Report of a Symposium, 2001; Koh Eng Chuan. Sex selection at birth. *Statistics Singapore Newsletter* V 17, January 1995; A.J. Coale. Excess female mortality and the balance of the sexes. *Population Development Review*, 1991; UN. *The World's Women 2000: Trends and Statistics*. NY: 2000; Elisabeth Croll, *Endangered Daughters: Discrimination and Development in Asia*. Routledge, 2000

Choosing sons/Endangering daughters Working Group on the Girl Child. *A Girl's Right to Live: Female Foeticide and Girl Infanticide*, 2007; Shuzhuo Li. "Imbalanced Sex Ratio at Birth and Comprehensive Intervention in China". UNFPA, 2007; Nancy Riley. *China's Population: New Trends and Challenges*. PRB, June 2004; Department of Social, Science & Technology, National Bureau of Statistics, National Bureau of Statistics of China. *Women and Men in China: Facts & Figures*, 2007

44–45 Part Four BODY POLITICS
Internet Pornography Statistics 2007, Techcrunch www.techcrunch.com/2007/05/12/internet-pornography-stats/

46–47 Breast Cancer
Breast cancer International Agency for Research on Cancer (IARC). *Globocan 2002: Cancer Incidence, Mortality & Prevalence*. Database IARC 2004, www-dep.iarc.fr/; Curado, M. P., Edwards, B., Shin. H.R., Storm. H., Ferlay. J., Heanue. M. and Boyle. P., eds (2007). *Cancer Incidence in Five Continents*, Vol. IX IARC Scientific Publications No. 160, Lyon, IARC; WHO. *WHO Mortality Database*, March 2007; WHO. *World Health Report 2004*, 2005

Breast cancer and race National Cancer Institute (USA). *SEER Cancer Statistics Review*, 2007. www.cancer.gov

Top five causes of cancer worldwide Parkin, D.M., et al. "Global cancer statistics 2002", *Cancer Journal for Clinicians*, 2005

48–49 HIV/AIDS
Living with HIV/AIDS The United Nations Joint Programme on HIV/AIDS (UNAIDS)/WHO. *Report on the Global AIDS epidemic*, 2006, http://data.unaids.org/pub/GlobalReport/2006/2006_GR_ANN2_en.pdf; UNAIDS/WHO. *AIDS Epidemic Update 2007*, http://data.unaids.org/pub/EPISlides/2007/2007_epiupdate_en.pdf

HIV/AIDS in Sub-Saharan Africa UNAIDS/WHO. *Report on the Global AIDS epidemic, 2006,* http://data.unaids.org/pub/GlobalReport/2006/2006_GR_ANN2_en.pdf; UNAIDS/WHO. *AIDS Epidemic Update 2007*, http://data.unaids.org/pub/EPISlides/2007/2007_epiupdate_en.pdf

Drug availability in Sub-Saharan Africa UNAIDS. *Report on the Global AIDS epidemic, 2006 – Treatment and Care*, p.7., http://data.unaids.org/pub/GlobalReport/2006/2006_GR_CH07_en.pdf

Orphaned by AIDS UNAIDS/WHO. *Report on the Global AIDS epidemic, 2006,* http://data.unaids.org/pub/GlobalReport/2006/2006_GR_ANN2_en.pdf

50–51 Sports
The Olympics: Athens, Summer 2004 International Olympic Committee. *Report: Women's Participation at the Games of the XXVIII Olympiad, Athens 2004, Annex 2*, February 2005, multimedia.olympic.org/pdf/fr_report_1000.pdf

Milestones International Olympic Committee, various reports

Gay Games personal correspondence, Federation of Gay Games

52–53 Beauty
The beauty beat www.missusa.com; www.globalbeauties.com/world/2007

Avon's world www.avoncompany.com/world/markets.html

Top five cosmetics companies annual company financial reports; news reports

Biggest cosmetic markets Market Insight: Key Trends & Developments in the global cosmetics and toiletries market. *Euromonitor International*, April 2007

Cosmetic surgery in the USA American Society for Aesthetic Plastic Surgery. *2007 Statistics*, www.surgery.org/press/statistics-2007.php

54–55 Under the Knife
Prevalence of female genital mutilation Office of the High Commissioner for Human Rights (OHCHR), UNAIDS, UNDP, United Nations Economic Commission for Africa (UNECA), United Nations Educational, Scientific and Cultural Organization (UNESCO), UNFPA, United Nations High Commissioner for Refugees (UNHCR), UNICEF, UNIFEM, WHO. *Eliminating female genital mutilation An interagency statement*, 2008; WHO. "Female genital mutilation" *Progress in Sexual and Reproductive Health*, 2006; WHO. Female Genital Mutilation, www.who.int/reproductive-health/fgm/index.html; UNICEF. *Changing a Harmful Social Convention: Female genital mutilation/cutting*, 2005

Legal status of FGM Center for Reproductive Rights. *Female Genital Mutilation, Legal Prohibitions Worldwide*, January 2008; WHO. Female Genital Mutilation, www.who.int/reproductive-health/fgm/index.html

A cultural practice PRB. *Abandoning Female Genital Cutting: Prevalence, Attitudes and Efforts to end the Practice*. Washington DC: 2001

56–57 Global Sex Trafficking
Sex Trafficking US State Department. *Trafficking in Persons Report*, June 2007, http://www.state.gov/documents/organization/82902.pdf; US Congressional Research Service. *Trafficking in Women and Children: The US and International Response,*

June 20, 2007, http://www.fas.org/sgp/crs/misc/RL30545.pdf; UN Office on Drug and Crime. *Trafficking in Persons Global Patterns*, http://www.unodc.org/pdf/crime/trafficking_persons_report_2006-04.pdf; International Organization for Migration (IOM). "Seduction, Sale and Slavery: Trafficking of Women and Children for Sexual Exploitation in Southern Africa." 3rd Edition, 2003

Mail order brides www.goodwife.com

58–59 Rape
Rape US State Department. *Country Reports on Human Rights Practices 2006 & 2007*, 2007 & 2008; Amnesty International. *Country Reports, 2007*; UN. *International Crime Survey*, 2000; UN News Centre, various reports; UN Womenwatch; WHO. *World Report on Violence and Health*, 2002; UN. Report of the Secretary-General, 2006. In-depth study on all forms of violence against women; UNIFEM. *Violence Against Women: Facts and Figures, 2007*; World Organization Against Torture (OMCT) 10 Reports, years 2003 and 2002; news and internet sources

Marital rape in law UNIFEM. *Not a Minute More: Ending Violence Against Women*, 2003; US State Department. *Country Reports on Human Rights Practices, 2006 & 2007*, 2007 & 2008

60–61 Part Five WORK
UNICEF. *The State of the World's Children, 2007*, 2006

62–63 Working for Wages
Women in the workforce International Labour Organization (ILO); UNDP. *Human Development Report 2008*; US Census Bureau. 2007 Current Population Survey; International Urban Training Centre (IUTC). "Global Gender Pay Gap" report, 2008

Child labor/Lost childhoods Plan International, UK. *Because I am a Girl*, 2007; UNICEF. *The State of the World's Children, 2007*

64–65 Workplaces
Industrial work ILO; UNDP. *Human Development Report, 2007–08*, http://hdr.undp.org/en/

Service work ILO; UNDP. *Human Development Report, 2007–08*, http://hdr.undp.org/en/

The hidden workforce ILO, Employment Sector. *Women and Men in the Informal Economy: A Statistical Picture*, Geneva: 2002; UNDP. *Human Development Report, 2007–08*, http://hdr.undp.org/en/

The global assembly line Jean-Pierre Singa Boyenge. *ILO database on export processing zones (Revised)*. Geneva: ILO, 2007; Lourdes Beneria. "Globalization and Gender: Employment Effects", workshop, Cairo 2005

66–67 Unequal Opportunities
Unemployment ILO. *Unemployment, underemployment and inactivity indicators (KILM 8-13)*, 2006; ILO. *Global Employment Trends*, 2007

Race and unemployment in South Africa Department of Labour, South Africa. *Women in the South African Labour Market 1995–2005*.

Women managers European Commission, DG EMPL. Database on women and men in decision-making; news reports; Australian Government. *Gender Income Distribution of Top Earners in ASX200 Companies*, 2006; ILO. *Breaking Through the Glass Ceiling*, 2004; Department of Labour, Republic of South Africa 2003 *Commission for Employment Equity Annual Report, 2001–02*; Catalyst. *2005 Catalyst Census of Women Corporate Officers and Top Earners of the Fortune 500*, 2006

Combining work and family ILO. *Breaking Through the Glass Ceiling*, 2004

Part-time workers ILO. *Women and Men in the Informal Economy*, 2002

Maternity leave The Clearinghouse on International Developments in Child, Youth and Family Policies at Columbia University. *Maternity, Paternity, and Parental Leaves in the OECD Countries, 1999–2002*; Catalyst. Maternity Leave in The US, Canada, Global, 2006

68–69 Farming
Agricultural work UNDP. *Human Development Report, 2007–08*, http://hdr.undp.org/en/; ILO, *Global Employment Trends*, 2007

Fish farmers The United Nations Food and Agricultural Organisation (FAO). Fisheries & Aquaculture Department. Facts on fish farming (aquaculture)

Gender division of labor in agricultural production FAO, Sustainable Development Division, www.fao.org/sd/WPdirect/WPre0112.htm

70–71 Unpaid Work
Women's Longer Day UNDP. *Human Development Report 2007–08*; Blackden, M & Q. Wodon. *Gender, Time Use, and Poverty in Sub-Saharan Africa*. World Bank Working Paper 73, 2006

Retirement time Eurostat. *Men and women in Europe*, 2008

Gender division of labor UNDP. *Human Development Report 2007–08*

Water carriers WHO & UNICEF. Joint Monitoring Programme on Water, www.wssinfo.org/en/welcome.html; UNDP. *Human Development Report 2006–07*. World Bank. *Development Outreach*, Spring 2001; Blackden, M & Q. Wodon. *Gender, Time Use, and Poverty in Sub-Saharan Africa*. World Bank Working Paper 73, 2006; UNFPA. *Global Population & Water*, 2003; UNICEF. *State of the World's Children, 2007*; World Bank. *Gender, Time Use & Poverty in Sub-Saharan Africa*, 2006

72–73 Migration

Migrant women workers from Asia United Nations, 2006b. *Trends in Total Migrant Stock: The 2005 Revision. CD-ROM Documentation*. Department of Economic and Social Affairs, Population Division; UNIFEM, 2006. *Empowering Women Migrant Workers*, 1 June 2006 (draft), UNIFEM. http://www.unifem.org/attachments/gender_issues/women_poverty_economics/WomenMigrantWorkersBrief20062007.pdf; UNIFEM, 2002. *Facts about Women's Migration for Work in Asia*. East and Southeast Asia Regional Office, http://www.unifem-eseasia.org/projects/migrant/03facts.pdf; ILO. International Labor Migration Database; Heyzer, Noleen, et al. *The Trade in Domestic Workers*. London: Zed, 1994; Sylvia Chant. *Gender and Migration in Developing Countries*. London: Bellhaven Press, 1992; Peter Stalker. *Workers without Frontiers*. ILO/Lynne Reiner Press, 2000; UN. *Women in a Changing Global Economy*. NY: UN, 1995

Major migrant-sending countries ILO. International Labour Migration Database; United Nations, 2006b. *Trends in Total Migrant Stock: The 2005 Revision. CD-ROM Documentation*. Department of Economic and Social Affairs, Population Division; United Nations, 2006a. *World Migrant Stock: The 2005 Revision Population Database*, Department of Economic and Social Affairs, Population Division,http://esa.un.org/migration/index.asp?panel=1

Global nurses Kingma, M. *Nurses on the Move: A Global Overview*. Health Services Research, 42:3, Part II (June 2007):1281-1298.

74–75 Part Six To Have and Have not

The World Bank. *World Development Indicators 2007*

76–77 Water

Water supplies WHO & UNICEF. Joint Monitoring Programme on Water, www.wssinfo.org/en/welcome.html; UNDP. *Human Development Report 2006–07*, hdr.undp.org/en/reports/global/hdr2006/; UNFPA. *Global Population & Water*, 2003; UNICEF. *State of the World's Children, 2007*

Sanitation shortfall WHO & UNICEF. Joint Monitoring Programme on Water, www.wssinfo.org/en/welcome.html; UNDP. *Human Development Report 2006–07*

The journey to water World Bank. *Gender, Time Use & Poverty in Sub-Saharan Africa*, 2006.

78–79 Literacy

Illiteracy UNESCO. *Global Education Digest, 2007*, http://www.uis.unesco.org/ev.php?ID=7002_201&ID2=DO_TOPIC; UNDP. *Human Development Report 2006–07*

Illiteracy trends UNESCO. Statistics Center.

Functional illiteracy in the USA US Department of Education. *National Assessment of Adult Literacy*, 2006; Statistics Canada & Organisation for Economic Co-operation and Development (OECD). *Learning a Living: First Results of the Adult Literacy and Life Skills Survey*

Gender differences Eurostat. European Commission. *The life of women and men in Europe – A statistical portrait*. Luxembourg: Office for Official Publications of the European Communities, 2008

80–81 School

Primary school enrolment UNESCO. *Global Education Digest*, 2007

Secondary schooling UNESCO Institute for Statistics. *Gender Parity in Education*, March 2008

Education and poverty in the USA US Census. pubdb3.census.gov/macro/032007/pov/new29_200_01.htm

82–83 Higher Education

University UNESCO. *Global Education Digest*, 2007; American Council on Education. *Fact Sheet on Higher Education*, 2007

Women teaching at tertiary level UNESCO. *Global Education Digest*, 2007

Tertiary education UNESCO. *Global Education Digest*, 2007

84–85 Wired Women

Online UNDP. *Human Development Report 2006*; International Telecommunications Union; US State Department Reports; Women and Global Science and Technology (WIGSTAT); www.internetworldstats.com/stats.htm

Computer users PEW. Global Attitudes Project, Truly a World Wide Web, Feb 2006

Race and gender online in the USA US National Telecommunications and Information Administration, http://www.ntia.doc.gov/reports/2008/Table_HouseholdInternet2007

Household internet access US National Telecommunications and Information Administration, http://www.ntia.doc.gov/reports/2008/Table_HouseholdInternet2007

86–87 Property

Property discrimination UNICEF. *State of the World's Children 2007*; ICRW. *Property Ownership for Women*, 2005; FAO. *Rural Women's Access to Land in Latin America, 2001*; FAO. Various reports, and *World Agricultural Census, 2001*

Home ownership in the USA US Census. *American Housing Survey, 2005*; US Census Bureau. Table 955, *Home Ownership Rates by Age and Household Type, 1985–2005*

88–89 Poverty

Living on the edge UNDP. *Human Development Report 2007–08*; Eurostat. *The social situation in the EU 2005–06*

Increasing poverty in Latin America CEPAL. *Social Panorama of Latin America, 2006*

Living in extreme poverty UNDP. *Human Development Report 2007–08*, http://hdrstats.undp.org/indicators/23.html

90–91 Debt

Indebtedness Past IMF Disbursements and Repayments for all members from May 01, 1984 to April 30, 2008, http://www.imf.org/external/np/fin/tad/extrep1.aspx; : http://www.bicusa.org/en/Article.92.aspx

Regional trends World Development Indicators online

Aid as proportion of GNI UNDP. *Human Development Report 2007–08*. Table 17.

92–93 Part Seven POWER

UN. Office of Special Advisor on Gender, various reports; UN. Report of the UN Secretary-General, Improvement of the status of women in the United Nations System, September 2004; Office of the Focal Point for Women

94–95 The Vote

Votes for Women Inter-Parliamentary Union (IPU); news reports; UNDP. *Arab Human Development Report, 2005*; Caroline Daley & Melanie Nolan. *Suffrage & Beyond: International Feminist Perspectives*. NY: NYU Press, 1994

96–97 Women in Government

Women in government IPU, www.ipu.org/wmn-e/classif.htm; US State Department. "Focus on Afghanistan", http://www.state.gov/g/wi/c6196.htm; US State Department. factsheet, "U.S. Commitment to Women in Iraq" Feb. 22, 2005, http://www.state.gov/g/wi/rls/42512.htm; US State Department. "Women in Iraq: Background and Issues for U.S. Policy" June 23, 2005, http://fpc.state.gov/documents/organization/64497.pdf; UNDP. *Human Development Report 2007–08*; news reports

Ministerial positions UNDP. *Human Development Report 2007–08*

98–99 Seats of Power

European Parliament IPU, www.ipu.org/wmn-e/regions.htm

Quotas for national parliament Institute of Democracy and Electoral Assistance. *Global Database of Quotas for Women*, www.quotaproject.org

Women heads of government IPU. "Women in Politics: 60 Years in Retrospect", http://www.ipu.org/PDF/publications/wmninfokit06_en.pdf; www.guide2womenleaders.com; news reports

Running the city UN/INSTRAW. "New Gender Machinery at the Local Level in Latin America," http://www.un-instraw.org/en/downloads/gender-governance-and-political-participation/index.php; Center for Women and Politics, Eagleton Institute of Politics, Rutgers, The State University of New Jersey, www.cawp.rutgers.edu/Facts/Officeholders/mayors-curr.html; Council of European Municipalities and Regions. "Women's Political Participation in CEMR Members", www.afccre.org/cms_file.asp?id=323; news reports

100–101 Crisis Zones

Crisis zones WHO. *Violence Against Women Living in Situations of Amred Conflict*, 2000; Human Rights Watch, various reports; World Organization Against Torture. *Violence Against Women. 10 Reports/Year 2001*. Geneva, 2002

Refugees UN Committee for Refugees, various reports; UNHCR, various reports; news reports

Rape in war zones News reports, including: *Congo* John Holmes. "Congo's rape war." *Los Angeles Times*, October 11, 2007, http://www.latimes.com/news/opinion/la-oe-holmes11oct11,0,6685881.story; *Colombia* http://www.peacewomen.org/resources/Colombia/OMCT2003.html; *Haiti* http://www.peacewomen.org/news/Haiti/Mar07/kidnap_rape.html; *Iraq* http://www.peacewomen.org/news/Iraq/July04/ordeal.html; *Kenya* recent article. "Mugumo Munen Women bear the brunt of conflict." *Sunday Nation*, Kenya, June 6, 2008, http://www.nationmedia.com/dailynation/nmgcontentry.asp?category_id=1&newsid=124917

102–103 Women in the Military

Armed forces NATO. Committee on Women in the NATO Forces, www.nato.int/issues/women_nato/index.html; Women's Research & Educational Institute, www.wrei.org/index.htm; US Department of Defense, various reports

Peacekeeping UN, Department of Peacekeeping Operations; UN, Womenwatch. "Facts and Figures on Women, Peace & Security", 2005

Homosexuality Center for the Study of Sexual Minorities in the Military; news reports

104–105 Feminisms

News reports

106–123 Part Eight WORLD TABLES

As cited.

Index